GLOB

TRA

GOA AND BOMBAY

ROBIN GAULDIE

NEW
HOLLAND

Jane Berry.

GLOBETROTTER
TRAVEL GUIDE

*** Highly recommended
** Recommended
* See if you can

First edition published in 1996
by New Holland (Publishers) Ltd.
London • Cape Town • Sydney • Singapore

24 Nutford Place
London W1H 6DQ
United Kingdom

80 McKenzie Street
Cape Town 8001
South Africa

3/2 Aquatic Drive
Frenchs Forest, NSW 2086
Australia

Copyright © 1996 in text: Robin Gauldie
Copyright © 1996 in maps: Globetrotter Travel Maps
Copyright © 1996 in photographs:
Individual photographers as credited
Copyright © 1996 New Holland (Publishers) Ltd

ISBN 1 85368 644 1

Commissioning Editor: Tim Jollands
Managing Editor: Sean Fraser
Editors: Susannah Coucher, Catherine Randall
Editorial Assistant: Rowena Curtis
Picture Researcher: Emily Hedges
Design and DTP: Kathryn Fotheringham
Cartographer: Desirée Oosterberg
Compiler/Verifier: Elaine Fick
Reproduction by cmyk prepress
Printed and bound in Hong Kong by South China
Printing Company (1988) Limited

Photographic Credits:
Jeanette Baker (Photobank), page 17; **David Beatty
(RHPL),** page 96; **Geoff Benson**, page 92; **Mark
Boekstein,** cover (top left and bottom right), title
page, page 7; **Gerald Cubitt**, cover (bottom left),
pages 10 (top), 19 (bottom), 26, 62, 67, 68, 70, 77, 93,
108; **Alain Evrard (RHPL)**, pages 19 (top), 52;
FootPrints, page 35; **Robert Harding**, pages 6, 9
(bottom), 10 (bottom), 36, 45 (bottom), 100, 101;
Nigel Gomm (RHPL), page 30; **Cecilia Innes**, page
15, 46 (top and bottom), 103; **Maurice Joseph
(RHPL)**, pages 29, 44, 49, 56, 63, 106 (bottom), 110
(top); **LifeFile**, pages 18; 24, 25, 28, 48, 50, 61 (top),
82, 85, 86, 89, 91, 98, 99, 102, 104, 106 (top), 112, 113,
120; **The Mansell Collection**, pages 13, 16; **Neil
McAllister**, 8, 12, 27 (top and bottom), 80 (top and
bottom), 105; **Oren Palkovitch (RHPL)**, page 33;
PictureBank, cover (top right) pages 4, 9 (top), 37,
87, 111; **Simon Reddy**, pages 14, 51, 59, 88, 110
(below); **Sassoon (RHPL)**, page 116; **Michael Short
(RHPL)**, 20, 21, 22, 23, 40, 43, 45 (top), 47, 60, 61
(bottom), 65, 73, 74, 75, 76, 78; **Chase Swift (RHPL)**,
page 79; **Travel Ink/Abbie Enock**, 11, 53, 64, 66, 90,
JHC Wilson (RHPL), pages 34, 119 (top).

Although every effort has been made to ensure
accuracy of facts, telephone and fax numbers in this
book, the publishers will not be held responsible for
changes that occur at the time of going to press.

Cover Photographs:
Top left: *Women dressed in colourful, traditional garb
sell their wares to tourists on the beach.*
Top right: *The tourism industry and the hotel develop-
ers have not yet discovered Palolem.*
Bottom left: *Peacocks run wild in the landscaped
grounds of the Bondla Wildlife Sanctuary.*
Bottom right: *Small and pleasant buildings, reflecting
their Portuguese influence, overlook the tranquil
Mandovi River in Colva.*
Title Page: *Sari-clad women bathe in the sea as the sun
sets on the fishing boats bobbing in the distance.*

CONTENTS

1
Introducing Goa

Goa is a state within a state, with a unique, four-century-old Portuguese heritage which sets it apart from its partners in the vast patchwork of cultures, traditions and religions that is modern India.

The finest beaches on the subcontinent, a climate which is at its best when the European winter is at its worst and a span of accommodation which ranges from the cheapest of guesthouses to the most luxurious of resort hotels, have made this state on the Arabian Sea one of the world's fastest-growing tropical tourist destinations, attracting many holiday-makers every year.

But Goa has far more to offer than the average beach resort. Golden sands, winter sunshine, superb seafood and low prices are merely the most obvious of its charms. An older, more exotic India exists side by side with the swimming pools and golf courses of Goa's modern hotels; an India where sacred cows amble sleepily down dusty village roads, where fishermen haul their wooden boats up onto beaches beside sun-bathing tourists and where villagers drive ox-drawn ploughs through muddy rice-fields in the shadow of holiday hotels. Compared with many other parts of India, Goa inflicts relatively little culture shock on the visitor experiencing the wonders and worries of the developing world for the first time. Certainly, most Goans do not enjoy the standard of living most Westerners take for granted but there is little of the obvious destitution which blights the streets of less fortunate regions of the Indian subcontinent.

TOP ATTRACTIONS

*** Old Goa: spectacular ruins of the first 16th-century Portuguese colonial capital.
*** Panaji: sleepy Portuguese-built town, Goa's state capital.
*** Anjuna: superb beach and cheerful village with a colourful weekly market.
*** Aguada: top beach for luxury resort hotels.
** Colva-Benaulim: Goa's longest, finest, least crowded beaches.

Opposite: *Colva Beach is one of the finest in southern Goa, with miles of clean sand.*

THE LAND
Mountains and Rivers

Goa lies on the west coast of India, looking out onto the Arabian Sea, just under 600km (372 miles) south of Bombay and bordered by the states of Maharashtra in the north and Karnataka to the south and east.

Compared with other Indian states, Goa is tiny – a strip of land 100km (62 miles) long and only 50km (30 miles) wide. Most of the coastal area is flat, but as you travel inland the country rises gradually to the increasingly rugged slopes of the **Sahyadri** mountain range which hems Goa in to the east, separating it from the high, dry plateau of Karnataka. Flowing out of this watershed, several rivers water the fertile lowlands and five wide estuaries are the major features of Goa's coastline. The most important of these, the **Zuari** and **Mandovi** rivers, cut across the centre of the state, meeting to form a wide bay which effectively cuts the coast in two.

Seas and Shores

Goa's state capital, **Panaji**, lies on the south shore of the Mandovi River, with the former Portuguese capital of **Old Goa** a few kilometres upriver. To the south, across the Zuari River, is the state's major port, railhead and industrial centre of **Vasco da Gama**, named after the great Portuguese navigator who was the first European to visit Goa.

Below: *Traditional fishing boats are pulled up along most Goan beaches.*

The most developed stretch of coast is north of the Mandovi River, where **Fort Aguada** – one of the original Portuguese bastions – has been transformed into a complex of luxury hotels. **Calangute**, a little further north, and **Baga**, its neighbour, have become a nexus of middle-level holiday development, with many medium-sized and medium-priced hotels. The next beach north, **Anjuna**, is still popular with independent travellers but seems poised to go the way of Calangute and Baga. **Chapora**, however, represents the northern limit of mainstream tourism and offers fairly basic accommodation. It is still more popular with the tribe of young independent travellers than with slightly older package holiday-makers.

North of the Chapora River, beaches are almost deserted apart from fishing boats and the most determined backpackers. The facilities are very basic indeed.

Above: *With more than 180 varieties of fish and shellfish in Goan waters, fishing is an important industry.*

South of Vasco da Gama and the airport, **Bogmalo** beach is a long crescent of sand shared by several upper- to middle-bracket hotels. To the south of this bay lies Goa's longest stretch of beach. The northern half of this 20km (12½ mile) length of sand is called **Colva** and the southern part is known as **Benaulim**. Colva is still largely undeveloped. Benaulim village, roughly midway along the beach, has become a bustling small resort and rapid growth seems inevitable.

Goa's far south, like the far north, is a refuge for those who wish to escape mainstream tourism, with lovely beaches at **Betul** and beyond the headland of Cabo de Rama at **Palolem**, the remotest beach in Goa.

Climate

Lying some 1200km (745 miles) south of the Tropic of Cancer, Goa has a tropical climate characterized by balmy weather for much of the year with heavy

GOA	J	F	M	A	M	J	J	A	S	O	N	D
AVERAGE TEMP. °C	25	26	27	29	30	28	26	26	26	27	27	27
AVERAGE TEMP. °F	76	77	78	84	85	84	77	77	77	78	78	78
HOURS OF SUN DAILY	10	12	12	10	10	1	1	4	5	6	10	10
DAYS OF RAINFALL	1	0	1	8	9	30	30	30	20	10	5	5
RAINFALL mm	2	0	4	17	18	500	890	340	277	122	20	30
RAINFALL in	-	-	.15	.9	.9	20	36	14	11	5	.1	1.2

Above: *Coconut palms, like these growing near Chapora, are an important crop plant.*

monsoon rains during the summer months. The best time of year to visit is between the middle of September and the end of February when daytime temperatures average around 27°C (80°F) with seven to nine hours of sunshine per day.

At this time of year **humidity** is quite low and night-time temperatures are cooler. From early March, the temperature starts to climb, and can rise as high as 35°C (95°F) in April and May. The **monsoon**, which begins in June, comes as a relief for local people after the hot, dry months of early summer, bringing welcome rain and lower temperatures. Goa can be at its most beautiful at this time of year, with the vivid green of newly sprouting rice in place of the bare red earth and parched vegetation of the dry season. Cloudy skies and heavy rain, however, are a powerful deterrent to most visitors. **Rainfall** is at its heaviest in July when Goa receives up to 90cm (36in) of rain in a single month. Travelling within India generally becomes more difficult during the rainy season and Goa is no exception. Road, rail and air travel schedules are prone to disruption. Strong winds and high seas also put most beaches off limits at this time of year. The rains slacken off through August and draw to an end in early to mid-September.

The other destinations in this guide have slightly different weather patterns. **Bombay** has a similar monsoon season, but is hotter all year round than Goa, with average maximum temperatures only dipping below 30°C (85°F) in August. Inland, **Maharashtra** is drier with cooler weather at higher altitudes. Coastal **Kerala** experiences the same weather pattern as Goa, but the high inland plateau of **Karnataka** escapes the heaviest monsoon rains and has slightly cooler day and night temperatures.

WHAT TO WEAR

Even in Goa, India's most relaxed state, beachwear should be worn only at beach resorts. Indians dislike visitors who display too much skin, and skimpy shorts and skirts are frowned on, especially when visiting places of worship. Away from the beach, choose light cotton garments. Long-sleeved shirts and trousers are preferable in areas where mosquitoes are a nuisance.

Plant Life

At least 3000 years of human settlement, intensive farming, and a fast-growing population mean much of Goa's landscape is man-made, leaving little space for large wild animals. Around the coast and tourist resort areas, almost all the land is under cultivation with **crops** such as **coconut** and **cashew**, **mango**, **pineapple** and **rice** pushing out the wild flowers. Many of the brilliant **flowers** which brighten

the gardens and balconies of Goanese homes and resorts are imports, such as the scarlet and purple bougainvillea, originally from Brazil, which flourishes everywhere. Most visitors arrive during the dry winter months, when anything which is not irrigated dies, and so miss the explosion of flowers and greenery which greets the first monsoon rains when they fall in June.

Wildlife

Birds and **butterflies** fare better than wild mammals. Gorgeously coloured butterflies float around hotel gardens, and palm plantations and flooded rice paddies attract many species of birds. Goa's birdlife is far too rich to list in detail here, but the most easily spotted include **white herons**, **cattle egrets** and other wading birds which stalk fish and frogs among the sprouting rice. Goa has at least five species of **kingfisher**, which are often seen perching on telephone wires overlooking rice fields. **Bee-eaters**, **rollers** and **shrikes** are also fond of perching on phone wires and on the branches of thorn trees. Other common birds include cheeky, raucous **mynahs** whose cackles, whoops and whistles are heard everywhere. Circling over fields, along the coast and anywhere where there is rubbish, you may spot white-fronted **brahminy kites** and **vultures** scavenging for food.

Top: *Much of Goa is covered by rice fields.*
Above: *Cashew nuts are fermented and distilled into a fiery spirit called* feni.

TEMPLE MONKEYS

Flocks of mischievous **macaque monkeys** inhabit many Indian temple precincts, especially those sacred to **Hanuman**, the monkey-god. They are usually harmless, but they may sometimes make a grab for a dangling bag or camera. Feeding them is not advisable, as they may bite.

HOLY COWS

All over India, small flocks
of white **cattle** amble freely
through the streets, browse
on patches of wasteland or
stroll along the beach.
   According to Hindu
custom, these sacred cows
and bulls may not be
harmed. Even the bulls
are harmless, with none
of the aggressive instincts
of European bullocks, but
sacred cattle are a frequent
obstruction to traffic.

Above: *The Slender Loris,
which is rather lima-like,
is found widespread in
Southern India.*
Below: *Cattle egrets, often
seen in fields and along
rivers, are among the
commonest Indian birds.*

Goa's countryside becomes wilder as you head inland
towards the Western Ghats (mountain range). In eastern
and southern Goa three wildlife reserves have been set
aside to protect what is left of the state's virgin forest and
wildlife. The **Bondla Wildlife Sanctuary**, not far from
Ponda in east central Goa, is the most accessible of these.
The **Bhagwan Mahaveer Sanctuary**, close to the eastern
state border with Karnataka, is perhaps the most spectacular and is dominated by the steep, wooded Western
Ghats range. Close to Goa's southern border, the **Cotigao
Sanctuary** has until recently
been the least accessible of
the three. All three reserves
offer superb birdlife, smaller
common mammals including
langur and **macaque monkeys**,
gaur (wild cattle) and **antelope**
including nilgai, sambar, and
chital. The parks also shelter
a few **elephant**, **leopard** and
even **tiger**, but only the luckiest
visitor is likely to spot them
even at a distance.

HISTORY IN BRIEF

Known under many different names, Goa has a rather chequered history stretching into the far distant past. Long before the arrival of the Portuguese, the control over Goa's valuable natural harbours was contested by Hindu and Muslim princes. The Portuguese arrived in the 15th century and so Goa became a Portuguese colony, unlike the rest of the sub-continent which formed part of the British Raj. Goa remained a Portuguese enclave until 1961.

Goa's first **Dravidian** people mixed with settlers from the north, firstly from the **Indus Valley**, then with the **Aryan** invaders who began to arrive in India around 1500BC. From around the 3rd century BC, Goa came under the control of a number of would-be empire builders as part of the region then known as the **Konkan**. By the 12th century it had become a distinct realm ruled by the **Hindu Kadamba** dynasty, with its capital, **Govalpuri**, on the banks of the Zuari River where the ruins of Goa Velha now stand. Its natural harbours also attracted traders from the Arab world, but very few reminders of this era survive, as later waves of invaders ruthlessly destroyed the palaces and temples of the land they conquered.

Above: *Sacred cows seem to enjoy Goa's perfect beaches as much as the tourists.*

ANCIENT TRADERS

The region was known to the ancient Greeks as **Nelkinda**, and appeared on the charts and accounts of far lands drawn up by the cartographer Ptolemy of Alexandria in the third century BC. Traders from the Arab and Persian cities of the Arabian Gulf, who knew it as **Sindabur**, were long established along the coast by the time the Portuguese arrived.

Below: *Fishing boats moored on the Mandovi where the first Portuguese navigators landed.*

The Muslims

Around the end of the 12th century, the Hindu states of northern India had been conquered by **Muslim Turks**, who built an empire which controlled much of northern India with its capital in Delhi. At first, this had little impact on affairs in the south but gradually the Muslim conquerors fell out amongst themselves. In the late 14th century, a fresh wave of **Turkish invaders led by the great Timur** destroyed the Delhi sultanate, making way for a host of small, independent Muslim and Hindu kingdoms.

In the south, the two most important of these were the Muslim **Bahmanis**, ruling an empire stretching across what is now Karnataka, and the Hindu **Vijayanagars**. For the next century, they were locked in a struggle for control of southwest India.

The Bahmanis first succeeded in ousting the last of Goa's Kadamba rulers some time in the first half of the 14th century, only to lose Goa to the Vijayanagars a quarter of a century later. Wars continued between the two kingdoms throughout the 15th century and in 1470 the Muslim general **Mahmud Gawan** finally drove the Vijayanagars out. The **Bahmani** empire broke up towards the end of the 15th century, and when the first Portuguese caravels sailed into the mouth of the Mandovi, they found near its mouth the thriving main seaport of a Muslim state called **Bijapur**, ruled by **Yusuf Adil Shah**.

The Portuguese

During the late 15th and early 16th centuries, the tiny Atlantic nation of Portugal launched an astonishing series of voyages of discovery in the east. The Muslim conquests of Palestine and Byzantium, completed in the mid-15th century, had cut Europe off from the wealth of Asia and Portuguese captains sought a new route around Africa.

In 1488 the navigator **Bartolomeo Dias** rounded the Cape of Good Hope to find himself in the open seas of the Indian Ocean. Ten years later, a fleet commanded by **Vasco da Gama** went even further, reaching Calicut (now Kozhikode) in Kerala. Later expeditions, in 1500 and 1502, strengthened Portugal's hand and the Raja of Cochin allowed Da Gama to build a fortress there in return for his help against the rival Raja of Calicut.

Above: *Portuguese Captain-General, Afonso de Albuquerque.*

The rajas of the Indian coast were eager to become allies of the new arrivals. Portuguese ships and cannon, far superior to those of local rulers, would be a mighty advantage in the never-ending wars with their Muslim neighbours and Hindu rivals. The Portuguese, meanwhile, were delighted to find that the ports of western India could – as they had hoped – give them access to the fantastically lucrative spice trade of India, Ceylon (Sri Lanka) and the East Indies (Indonesia).

In 1510, the greatest of Portugal's commanders, **Afonso de Albuquerque**, arrived with a fresh fleet. With the connivance of the Raja of Vijayanagar and the local Hindus who, in fact, resented Muslim rule, Albuquerque swept into Goa and in 10 months of hard fighting on land and sea drove out the forces of the Adil Shah to raise the Portuguese flag.

With Goa secured, Albuquerque pushed on east, conquering Malacca on the Malaysian peninsula. Later, Portuguese admirals added possessions in the

THE EMPIRE BUILDER

Afonso de Albuquerque was the architect of Portugal's overseas empire. Within 10 years of Dias rounding Africa, Afonso had established Portuguese strongholds on the East African coast. By 1510 Goa was his. A year later he conquered Malacca, on the west coast of Malaysia, then sailed on east to seize Macau, in southern China. Fifteen years after his arrival, Portuguese ships had driven the Arabs from the Indian Ocean and the King of Portugal claimed to be 'Lord of the Conquest, Navigation and Commerce of Ethiopia, Arabia, Persia and India'.

Above: *Statue of Vasco da Gama overlooks the cathedrals of Old Goa.*

East Indies, Ceylon and Macau, while others consolidated Portuguese control of a chain of territories stretching all the way around Africa. Goa became known as 'Goa Doirada' or '**Golden Goa**' and it was the most important link in this chain. Albuquerque set out to turn Goa into a mirror image of Portugal, importing priests to convert the Goanese to the Catholic faith and encouraging his soldiers and settlers to marry the local women and found a new nation loyal to Portugal. This racially enlightened policy was maintained throughout the years of Portuguese rule and undoubtedly played a major part in contributing to the easy-going Goa of today.

Portugal's first territories – the central provinces of Ilhas, Bardez, and Salcete – are still known as the **Old Conquests**. Much later, in the 17th and 18th centuries, the Portuguese added the provinces of Bicholim, Sanguem, Ponda, Quepem and Canacona which became known as the **New Conquests**. By the mid-17th century the Portuguese capital, now known as Velha Goa, was one of the marvels of the East, a glittering capital to rival Lisbon and outshine Paris or London.

European rivals

New European rivals were beginning to appear in Indian waters; first the **Dutch**, then the **French** and then lastly the **British**. For the next century Britain, France and their Indian allies battled for control of the subcontinent. By the end of the 18th century Britain had ousted France. With the defeat of the great Indian uprising of 1857–1858 (still sometimes referred to as the Indian Mutiny) the British Raj was supreme from the Himalayas to Cape Comorin and remained so until its partition into independent India and Pakistan in 1947.

These momentous events largely passed Goa by, though it was occupied by the British between 1799–1813. Portugal was unable to keep up its imperial impetus, and its scattered empire languished. 'Golden Goa' went into decline as a succession of plagues rather than wars killed many of its people and in the early 19th century the capital moved to Panjim (now known

---

HOLY ORDERS

Old Goa's churches were founded and controlled by several different **Catholic** orders, all of which followed the Portuguese flag east in search of converts. They set up their headquarters in the colonial capital. The first to reach Goa were the **Franciscans**, who arrived soon after Albuquerque's conquest of the city and built their first convent in 1517.

In 1835, a newly liberal Portuguese government ordered the dissolution of the religious orders in Portuguese territories, and many of the buildings of Old Goa were abandoned.

HISTORICAL CALENDAR

973AD Goa first appears in historical records as Gove or Gopakkapattana, capital of the Kadamaba King Shastadeva I.

14th century Muslim expansion into southern India.

1325 Muhammad bin Tughluq Sultan of Delhi. Gopakkapattana sacked by Muslim invaders.

1345–1470 Goa disputed by Kadamba, Bahmani and Vijayanagar kingdoms.

1490 Bahmani empire disintegrates. Goa passes to Yusuf Adil Shah of Bijapur.

1498 Vasco da Gama's fleet arrives in Calicut.

1500–1502 Portuguese expeditions continue to arrive in India.

1510 Afonso de Albuquerque, Portuguese Captain-General, seizes Goa from the Adil Shah.

Later 16th century Portuguese consolidate hold on Goa, expand eastwards. 'Golden Goa' becomes capital of Portuguese overseas empire.

1795 Portuguese Viceroy moves residence from Velha Goa to Panaji.

1763 Portuguese seize Cabo de Rocha island.

1781 Bicholim conquered by Portuguese.

1782 Portuguese conquer Satari, from native ruler.

1791 King of Sunda cedes Ponda, Sanguem, Quepem and Canacona by treaty.

1799–1813 British occupy Goa to deny it to France.

1818–1858 British Raj gradually expands over entire Indian subcontinent.

1947 British India partitioned into Pakistan and India. Goa remains under Portuguese rule.

1948 Nehru makes first demand for return of Goa to India.

1961 Indian forces invade Goa. Portugal surrenders.

1961–87 Goa directly ruled from New Delhi.

1987 Goa achieves statehood within India.

as Panaji). Portuguese neutrality kept Goa out of both world wars and made Panaji a hotbed of espionage by both Allied and Axis agents during World War II.

Union with India

The rest of India achieved independence from Britain in 1947, and the Indian government immediately demanded that Goa too should become part of the newly independent state. The Portuguese government refused, and over the next 14 years relations between the two countries deteriorated until, on 17 December 1961, Prime Minister **Jawaharlal Nehru** ordered Indian forces to invade the Portuguese enclave. Faced with overwhelming force, the Portuguese surrendered without resisting on 19 December, and after four and a half centuries of Portuguese rule, Goa became part of the Republic of India.

Below: *The Portuguese colonial legacy includes gracious old-fashioned family homes.*

Most of the agitation for Goa to be absorbed into India came from **Indian nationalists** outside the province. Within Goa, many of the large Portuguese-speaking Christian minority were less enthusiastic. Under Portuguese rule they controlled most of Goa's trade and industry and the lower ranks of its bureaucracy. They were reluctant to see Goa absorbed into one of the much larger neighbouring states, and they feared that an influx of carpet-baggers would deprive them of their privileged social status.

Happily, **independence** proved mainly beneficial to Goa. The Portuguese were not great believers in overseas investment, and in fact were actively opposed to modernization. At the end of the colonial era Goa still lacked most of the amenities of the 20th century. There were no tarred roads or electricity outside Panaji, no airport, no modern port facilities, and virtually no telephone or telegraph system. There were no public health facilities, the education system was rudimentary, and there was practically no industry or modern farming.

Goa was a somnolent backwater isolated not only from the rest of India but from most of the outside world. Union with India brought substantial planned investment and modernization. This included a road and telecommunications network which now embraces all of Goa's main towns and villages; new bridges to span the state's rivers; a public health, education and welfare system; new farming techniques; better port facilities and the beginnings of an industrial infrastructure.

MAHATMA MOHANDAS GANDHI

Gandhi was born in 1869, the son of the prime minister of the small state of **Porbandar**. He studied law in London, then worked as a lawyer in South Africa until the age of 46. On his return to India, he became a leader of the independence movement, preaching non-violence. He abandoned European garb for the cotton *dhoti* and won the title 'Mahatma' (Great Soul) from his followers. He led India to independence in 1947, only to be assassinated the following year by a Hindu fanatic who was outraged by Gandhi's rejection of the caste system.

The Latest Invasion

Perhaps the biggest single factor in dragging Goa into the modern world has been the opening of **Dabolim airport**, first to internal flights linking Goa with Bombay and Delhi and then to international charter flights. Until direct charter flights from Europe began in the 1980s, most foreign visitors to Goa were either low-budget independent travellers in search of hippy heaven or relatively wealthy tourists combining a stay in a luxury beach hotel with a tour of the historic sights of northern India. The internationalization of Dabolim airport brought in a new breed of middle-income holiday-maker and made Goa a holiday destination in its own right, quite independent of the attractions of the north. The number of foreign visitors increased from 8371 in 1973 to 170,658 in 1993. More than half of these are from the UK and around 15% come from Germany. At the same time, Goa has become quite a fashionable holiday destination for Indians too, attracting almost 800,000 Indian tourists in 1993.

JAWAHARLAL MOTILAL NEHRU

Gandhi's successor was very different. A western-influenced aristocrat with the common touch, he was committed to making India a mechanized modern society and to raising living standards. The true architect of modern India, he dominated politics until his death in 1964, founding a political dynasty which dominated Indian politics until the assassination of his grandson, Rajiv Gandhi, by Tamil extremists in 1990.

Opposite: *Mahatma 'Great Soul' Mohandas Gandhi.*
Below: *Hotel Cidade de Goa stands on its own beach close to Panaji.*

GOVERNMENT AND ECONOMY

Since 1987 Goa has been a fully fledged state of the Republic of India, electing its own state assembly which has control over the police, the education system, agriculture and industrial matters. Goa also elects its own members of the two houses of the national parliament in New Delhi.

India's governmental system is parliamentary, with a 500-member lower house called the **Lok Sabha** (House of the People) and a 250-member upper house called the **Rajya Sabha** (Council of States). The two houses, together with the state assemblies, elect a figurehead president but the reins of power are in the hands of the prime minister.

Economic Development

The obvious poverty which almost always strikes the first-time visitor masks the fact that India has become the world's 10th largest industrial power. Until recently Indian governments have placed their faith in a centrally planned, protectionist economy, with a series of five-year plans aimed at modernizing various sectors. At national and state level, government – and a cumbersome bureaucracy – play a big part in every aspect of economic life. In recent years liberalization of the economy has allowed more overseas imports and permitted increased competition with state-owned companies. There are also attempts to develop new, high-technology industries in place of outmoded heavy industry.

Left: *Most Indians work on the land – such as these women at work in the fields at Cortalim.*
Below: *Fishing trawlers crowd the harbour at Panaji. Much of their catch is exported.*

Industry and Agriculture

Despite all this, most Indians make their living from the land, as they always have. This is especially true in Goa, which has very little industry apart from the extensive open-cast **mining** operations around Bicholim, in central Goa. The state produces around 30% of India's **iron ore**, most of it exported through the port of Marmagao at the mouth of the Zuari. **Tourism** is poised to become an even more important foreign currency earner. **Fishing** is quickly being industrialized, and canned sardines and frozen shellfish have become important export items. This probably means that Goa's small-boat fishermen are doomed and the days of cheap prawns and lobster are numbered.

Coconuts, cashews and rice are Goa's staple **crops**. Most of Goa's rice is grown in the fertile, low-lying land of the Old Conquests, with planting occurring both during the monsoon and in the dry winter season. Coconuts and cashews are very important, with almost half of the state's cultivated land devoted to one or the other.

THE PEOPLE

With a population of around 1.2 million, Goa is a drop in India's ever-increasing ocean of more than 850 million people. As a result, articulate Goanese often feel that their state has little chance of making itself heard in New Delhi or getting positive results from the Government of India – a view often put forward stridently in the local press.

Though **Portuguese** is no longer very widely spoken, the influence of four centuries of Portuguese colonial rule is still strong, and Portuguese surnames like Mascarenhas or D'Souza are common amongst the state's older Christian families and in the business, political and academic elite.

Just over 30% of Goa's people are Christians, most of them **Roman Catholics**, and the state is dotted with Christian churches. In general, most of Goa's Christians are found in Panaji and along the coast, which historically is the area of the greatest Portuguese influence. Here, there seem to be churches at every turn, most of them built on the site of earlier temples and mosques razed by the Portuguese. Despite the high profile of the

Opposite: *Laden with brightly coloured fabrics and jewellery, women often haggle with the holidaymakers on Goa's beaches.*
Below: *Ice cream vendors pedal their wares around the city streets and on resort beaches.*

Christian community, proportionally by far the biggest of any Indian state, most of Goa's people are **Hindus**. They predominate in the inland rural communities, and the visitor is far more likely to spot the characteristically colourful Hindu temples in locations well away from the coast. Ethnic and religious frictions are quite rare – perhaps because the two main communities are geographically separate.

Visitors arriving in Goa from other parts of India are often pleasantly surprised by the rather reserved friendliness of most Goans. There is very little of the frenzied hassle and hard sell

which plagues the tourist circuit of northern India. Local people, however, are divided in their feelings about the flood of **tourism** which is now pouring into their once-quiet backwater. The first visitors to arrive in numbers were the hippies of the 1960s, who found in Goa a tranquil resting place after the rigours of overland travel. Many of Goa's less-accessible beaches are still favoured by alternative travellers, whose sex, drugs and rock and roll lifestyle is disliked by local conservatives – and by tourism developers who fear the hippies deter the more lucrative package holiday-makers.

Meanwhile, runaway tourism development has also been accused by local and international pressure groups of driving villagers off their land, destroying the livelihood of local fisherfolk and polluting beaches and the sea. The debate continues, but the tourism boom shows no signs of slackening.

CASTE SYSTEM

There are many sub-castes, but Hinduism is mainly dominated by four castes: **Brahmins**, or priests; **Kshatriyas**, or warriors and rulers; **Vaisyas** or merchants and farmers; and **Sudras** or artisans and manual workers. The hierarchy is rigid, with no way of changing caste.

Outside the caste system are the widely oppressed people called 'untouchables' – because their touch, or even their shadow, is believed to defile upper-caste people. Gandhi sought to improve their position, calling them the '**Harijans**' (Children of God).

Above: *Bombay, India's film capital, churns out thousands of blockbusters every year.*

Language

India's official language is **Hindi**, the mother tongue of around half the country's people, but in a country of so many different races and ethnic groups there are literally hundreds of regional languages and dialects.

Hindi is most widely spoken in northern India, and central government efforts to make it the sole national language of government and education have become a hot political issue down south.

Southern states have stubbornly resisted the sidelining of their own more widely used languages, which are descended from the **Dravidian** tongue of the first dwellers in the region. The most widespread of these is **Tamil**, spoken in the southeast. To the south and east of Goa, the main languages are **Kannada**, **Telugu** and **Malayalam**.

All over India, but especially in the south, **English** is a vital second language and is universally spoken in government, business circles and the tourism industry.

India has scores of English-language newspapers, including the country's most influential, *The Times of India*. In conversation with each other, Indians often switch with ease from English into Hindi or other regional languages. English-language newspaper stories and everyday speech are spiced with Hindi expressions which can make conversation hard to follow.

With British tourists accounting for more than half the foreign visitors to Goa, English is even more popular. Almost everyone you are likely to meet in shops, hotels, and restaurants will speak enough English for you to get by. Taxi drivers usually speak some English, and railway personnel are usually quite fluent. This is true also in the main towns and beach resorts of neighbouring Kerala and Karnataka, where many people speak basic English.

Out in the countryside, though, it's a different story. In northern Goa, people may speak **Marathi**, the language of the neighbouring Maharashtra state. Goa's own language, **Konkani**, has been recognized as an independent tongue since 1976 and is widely spoken.

Portuguese, on the other hand, has died out quite rapidly since 1961, and survives mainly in the kitchen and on restaurant menus, where peculiarly Goan-Portuguese dishes have survived the demise of the Portuguese empire.

In the next-door state of Karnataka, which sees far fewer foreign tourists, English is not widely spoken outside the major cities of Mysore and Bangalore and the most widely used language is **Kannada**.

In Kerala, to the south, English is much more widely spoken. A series of Marxist state governments committed to education have given the state the highest literacy rate in India at more than 60%, close to double the national average.

Malayalam, Kerala's main language, is closely related to Tamil, the largest language group in southern India and the main language of Tamil Nadu state, which occupies India's southwest tip.

Below: *Produce piled high in one of Goa's busy markets.*

INDIAN EPICS

India's two greatest epics are the Ramayana and the Mahabharata. **Ramayana** tells the story of an eons-long war between Rama and his allies and Ravana, the demon-king of Lanka. In the **Mahabharata** story, five good brothers, with the help of Krishna, battle against 100 evil cousins and their demon helpers. Together with the Bhagavad Gita (the greatest of the Hindu sacred texts), and the Vedas, Upanishads and Puranas, these form the basis of the Hindu faith and all Hindu poetry.

Religion

India's history stretches back 4000 years, and each wave of people migrating into the subcontinent has brought a new faith or added to an existing one. Most Indians follow the **Hindu** faith, but there are sizable minorities of other nationalities, most notably **Muslims** (around 80 million) and **Sikhs** (around 15 million) with smaller minorities of **Buddhists** (around five million) and **Jains** (around three million).

Goa does not reflect the national picture. Most of its people (more than 60%) are Hindu, but Christians, who are a tiny minority in most other Indian states, are the second largest group (almost 40%). Muslims make up only 3% of the population. As a result, Goa has escaped the occasional clashes between Hindus and Muslims, Hindus and Sikhs, or between all three, which mar Indian politics.

Hinduism

Hinduism is the oldest and most complex faith in the world. India's first civilization, in the Indus Valley, held early Hindu beliefs. The Aryan invaders who started to arrive around 1500BC added new gods to the already extensive pantheon and created the complex caste system which survives more or less intact today.

With its dozens of deities, many of whom have several different personalities, Hinduism can be baffling to the outsider. In a sense, however, each Hindu god can be seen as just one aspect of a single supreme being.

There are three major deities: Brahma, the creator; Vishnu, the preserver; and Shiva, who represents destruction and rebirth. All-seeing **Brahma**, the most distant of the gods, is shown with four faces, often accompanied by his consort **Sarasvati**, the goddess of wisdom, riding a white swan. **Shiva** is often represented by the stone lingam, and is depicted riding a bull and bearing a trident. One of his aspects is **Nataraja**, the dancer who created the world. His consort, **Parvati**, is the great beauty

of the Hindu pantheon. She has two less charming sides to her nature: **Kali**, the death-goddess, with her girdle of human skulls, and **Durga**, the goddess of destruction, multi-limbed, armed and mounted on a tiger.

Vishnu is perhaps the most human of the gods, appearing on Earth in a series of incarnations symbolizing the nine ages of the Earth. Vishnu rides the mighty Garuda bird and his consort is **Lakshmi**, goddess of wealth and prosperity. In his first six incarnations he appeared as a wild boar or a manticore (half-man, half-lion). In his seventh he appeared as **King Rama**, leader of mankind and the gods against the demons in Hinduism's most accessible epic, the Ramayana. In his eighth, he came as the playful **Krishna**, brought up by shepherds and famed for his romps with pretty shepherdesses. In paintings and temple carvings he is coloured blue and plays the flute.

Hinduism also has a large supporting cast of lesser deities, like Krishna's faithful sidekick **Hanuman**, the monkey god, and **Ganesha**, the elephant-headed son of Shiva and Parvati and god of wisdom and wealth; part of the religion's age-old appeal is the existence of a god to turn to in every aspect of everyday life, from bringing up children to catching fish, planting rice or investing money. Also appealing is the notion of rebirth: things may not be so great as a poor rice farmer in this life, but there is always the possibility of reincarnation as a wealthy man in the next life, or the one after that.

Above: *Hindu temples, like this one at Margao, are usually brightly painted and scented with aromatic essences.*
Opposite: *Hindu holy men called* sadhus *perform seemingly miraculous feats at traditional festivals.*

HINDU TEMPLES

A typical Hindu temple is a riot of colour, with a many-tiered spire encrusted with brilliantly painted gods, demons, and mythical creatures. Inside, incense burns in front of garlanded images or phallic Shiva lingams. Offerings of rice are often made, and you will probably be asked to contribute a small sum to the upkeep of the temple. Old and disabled people often beg outside temples. Should you wish to give, have a pocketful of small change ready.

Christianity

Vasco da Gama told the Indians of the Malabar coast
(now Kerala) that he had come seeking 'Christians and
spices'. He found both, for southern India is the site of
the world's oldest Christian community, founded by **St
Thomas the Apostle** in AD52 and boosted by the arrival
of Christian merchants from the Levant towards the
end of the 2nd century AD.

The **Portuguese** imposed Christianity on Goa by the
sword and by conversion. Their assault on Islam was
ruthless. Goa's Muslim inhabitants were slaughtered
or driven into exile and mosques were razed. Their
approach to the Hindus was less violent. Many converts
came from the lower castes or the Dalit community.
Catholicism offered them a way out of the rigid caste
system, or so it seemed, while its pantheon of the Holy
Trinity, the Virgin Mary, and a colourful array of saints
and apostles must have seemed not too different from
the familiar Hindu pantheon. The Portuguese did, however, destroy Hindu temples in the Old Conquests. By
the 18th century they had become less destructive, and
Goa's oldest temples are located in the New Conquest
provinces which spent less time under Portugal.

Below: *Statue of Jesus
facing the Se Cathedral,
Old Goa.*

The Arts

The performing arts in India today are part of a continuous artistic tradition stretching back into antiquity. From the earliest times Indian artists have been masters of the plastic arts, producing superbly graceful and dignified stone images of gods, kings and

dancers. Ancient temples and holy caves are decorated with fluid frescoes, often depicting scenes from the great Hindu epics, the **Ramayana** and the **Mahabharata**. Modern artists too are still strongly influenced by the colours, the strong lines, and above all the narrative tradition embodied in traditional Hindu art, in which every picture tells a story, with more than 3000 years of complex myths and legends to draw on.

Above: *Earthenware pots are in everyday use in the kitchens of India.*
Below: *Embroidered textiles are treasured in many Indian homes and make wonderful souvenirs of a visit to Goa.*

   Music and **dance** are equally closely involved with Hindu beliefs. There are dances from every part of India, and for every occasion. Male and female dancers rarely if ever appear together, and in many dances, female roles are performed by men. Many dances tell stories of the gods and their battles with demons or encounters with mortals. Rama's prowess in the Ramayana, or Krishna's flirtations with mortal maidens, are popular themes of traditional dance.

   Goa's cultural heritage blends four centuries of Portuguese influence with an even older Indian musical and dramatic tradition. Unique to the state is the **felo**, a village play with song, music and dance which often weaves in local themes and satire. Portuguese musical instruments, like the fiddle and the guitar, have also been added to the local repertoire, and Goans still sometimes perform the mournful **fado** songs

Above: *Kathakali dancers in Kochi prepare for a performance by applying layers of their vividly coloured make-up.*

of Lisbon and Oporto. The rhythms of the Old Conquests, too, are unmistakably Iberian rather than Indian.

India's **movie** industry is one of the world's biggest, with a huge and voracious audience awaiting each new Hindi epic. Stars have godlike status, and several actors – male and female – have gone on to become leading politicians at state and national level, swept to power by the votes of millions of adoring cinema fans.

Most Indian films are made in the giant studios of Bombay, often nicknamed 'Bollywood'. Stars and directors work hard, often filming several movies simultaneously, and the output is phenomenal.

Plots are simple and melodramatic, with a romantic male and female lead, an obvious villain, and a stock supporting cast. Happy endings are the norm, but it's not unusual for the heroine to die tragically in the last reel. The entire cast breaks into song and dance at every opportunity, even in all-action productions, and since most Hindi epics run to about three hours, watching one can be an emotionally draining experience.

Food and Drink

Goa has some of the finest food in India, and its cuisine is less intimidating to inexperienced western palates than that of some other Indian states.

Seafood, including all sorts of fish and prawns, figure high on the menu, though the delicious tiger prawns and langouste which used to be such an affordable delight should be on the endangered list – they command high prices abroad and most of the catch is frozen for export. The commonest **fish** is the *bangra*, similar to a large sardine, which may be served freshly grilled, simmered

WINES

Imported wines, found only in upmarket hotels, are usually overpriced and of indifferent quality. Grapes are grown on the higher, cooler country of the **Karnataka** plateau around Hyderabad, which has an almost Californian climate. You may find locally made wines in some restaurants. In general, Indian white wines (if served very cold) are better than the reds.

Indian sparkling wine, sold in Goa under the **Pompadour** label, is good enough for export and is marketed in the UK and elsewhere as **Omar Khayyam**.

in a spicy tomato sauce, or in many other ways. Crispy fried pomfret, a small flatfish, is a favourite snack.

Pork, which is found nowhere else in India – both Hindus and Muslims consider the pig an unclean animal – is eaten with relish by the Christian Goans, usually generously flavoured with garlic. Other meats on the menu include mutton and sometimes goat. More westernized tourist restaurants will also serve steaks or hamburgers.

Like every Indian region, Goa has its own special **curry** dishes. The Goan version of vindaloo, called *vindalhao*, features pork simmered in garlic, vinegar and chillies. Many dishes are served *reichado*, stuffed with chillies and other spices. *Cabidel* is a favourite spicy pork stew, and *xacati*, chicken served with coconut-flavoured rice, is another spicy dish.

Everything comes with rice – though in the more tourist-oriented restaurants french fries are usually offered as an option – and main dishes are usually accompanied by flapjack-like *chapatis* or flat nan bread, originating in northern India but now found everywhere.

Off the tourist trail, one of the best bets throughout India is to order a *thali*, a vegetarian set meal featuring various kinds of *dal* (lentil stew), pickles, and curds.

SPIRITS AND BEERS

Goa's own tipple, **feni**, is made from the fermented sap of the coconut palm or from the fermented juice of the cashew nut. A clear, fiery spirit, it is an acquired taste which few visitors in fact find appealing. More palatable are the various Indian rums (all gold or dark) and whiskies. The best are blends of Scotch malt with local spirit. Beers include the excellent **Kingfisher**, in large 750ml bottles, and a variety of expensive imports.

Below: *Each Indian dish requires a unique blend of colourful spices, sold in bulk in every street market.*

2
Bombay:
Gateway to Goa

A huge, sprawling metropolis of more than 10 million people, Bombay is India in miniature, with all its colour, noise, and extremes of wealth and poverty. 'Bombay is a crowd,' writes Naipaul. 'Such a torrent of people swept across the road, in such a bouncing froth of light-coloured lightweight clothes, it seemed that some kind of invisible sluice-gate had been opened, and that if it wasn't closed again the flow of road-crossers would spread everywhere, and the beaten-up red buses and yellow-and-black taxis would be quite becalmed, each at the centre of a human eddy.'

With its blocks of grimy apartment buildings and offices, brightened by the garishly painted signboards of shops and businesses, Bombay is not a pretty city, but it vibrates with the urban urgency of millions of people in motion, day or night.

Recently redubbed **Mumbai** – its original Marathi name – by the Hindu fundamentalist government of Maharashtra state, Bombay is cosmopolitan in the truest sense of the word and is home to people from all over India and indeed all over the world. Sheer weight of numbers, and the head-spinning contrasts of grimy bazaars and elegant shops, squalid slums and five-star hotels, temples, mosques and brand new office blocks, can overwhelm the visitor.

Bombay grew up on a group of marshy islets off the coast of **Gujarat**. Given to Portugal in 1534 by the Sultan of Gujarat, it passed to Britain as the dowry of the Portuguese princess Catherine de Braganza, wife of Charles II, and in

DON'T MISS

*** **Prince of Wales Museum:** one of the finest collections of Indian art in the world in a splendid historic building.
*** **Elephanta Caves:** magnificent carvings and frescoes in temples carved into the rock.
** **Gateway of India:** splendid stone arch and relic of the heyday of the British Raj.

Opposite: *The Gateway of India, on Bombay's seafront, is a picturesque relic of the British Raj.*

1668 was leased to the British East India Company. Under British rule it grew to become the biggest seaport on the west coast of India. The opening of the **Suez Canal** in 1869 gave the already thriving city a further economic boost. Bombay had the greater advantage over Calcutta as it was closer to the European markets. On independence, it became the state capital of **Maharashtra**.

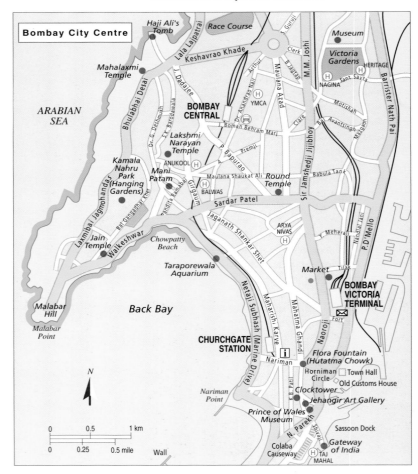

Bombay City Centre

Over the centuries, Bombay's islands have merged into one large, roughly triangular island, about 60km (37½ miles) long, broadest at its northern end, and tapering to a narrow southern tip, the **Colaba Causeway**. The heart of the city is built on the northern end of this narrow promontory, with the harbour to the east. **Marine Drive** (Netaji Subhash Road), the main city esplanade, sweeps northwest along the shore of Back Bay on the west side of the island. Malabar Point shelters Back Bay from the open sea to the west and is crowned by **Malabar Hill**, the city's most expensive residential district. Running parallel to Marine Drive, **Mahatma Gandhi Road** is the location of most of Bombay's historic public buildings and cuts through the heart of the city. This part of Bombay clearly shows its colonial heritage, with a collection of grand Georgian and Victorian Gothic buildings bequeathed by the British and still in use. Among the most imposing are the University, easy to find with its 80m (262ft) clock-tower overlooking KB Patil Marg, and the nearby High Court Building, built in 1878. Older buildings on Horniman Circle include the city's original Town Hall, opened in 1833, and the even older Customs House dating from 1720.

South of the city centre, the Colaba Causeway area is a mix of cheap accommodation and restaurants, shops and market stalls stretching south to the tip of the island.

Below: *Bombay markets overflow with vividly coloured fruit and vegetables, but no picture can convey the intoxicating smells of herbs and spices.*

ZOROASTRIANS

The Zoroastrians or Parsis of Bombay are among the last communities of a religion which once had believers throughout western Asia and the Mediterranean. Founded by the prophet *Zarathustra* (Zoroaster) in ancient Persia around the 7th century BC, Zoroastrianism revolves around belief in a single benevolent god, *Ahura Mazda*, in perpetual conflict with the evil spirit Ahriman.

Opposite: *Modern tower blocks mingle with old-fashioned buildings along Bombay's waterfront esplanade.*
Below: *The grandiose Victoria Terminus, built in the heyday of the British Empire, is the largest railway station in India.*

MARINE DRIVE (NETAJI SUBHASH ROAD)

Bombay's long crescent esplanade stretches from **Nariman Point** at its southeast end to **Malabar Point**, on the opposite side of **Back Bay**. The best way to see the city's main sites is either to book a taxi through your hotel for the day or, more cheaply, to take the half-day guided tour operated by the Maharashtra Tourist Development Corporation. **Flora Fountain** (Hutatma Chowk), at the south end of **Mahatma Gandhi Road**, is the focal point of the downtown business district and the starting point for most guided or independent explorations of the city. Around it are substantial 19th-century buildings evocative of the last days of the Raj. The most impressive is the Gothic Victoria Terminus, India's largest railway station. With its cathedral-like spires, turrets and arched windows it typifies the grandiose architecture of the British in India.

At its northern end, above the city's busy, colourful and grubby Chowpatty Beach, Marine Drive becomes Walkeshwar Road, running down the inner side of Malabar Point. At the southern end of this road, the **Jain Temple** is an unmistakable landmark, its onion-like spire glittering with thousands of mirror mosaic tiles and its walls covered with elaborate carvings.

Taraporewala Aquarium **

Midway along Marine Drive, you'll come across this fascinating aquarium, the largest in India, with displays of both freshwater and saltwater specimens. The emphasis here is on large sea-creatures rather than pretty ones. Sharks, rays, and marine turtles can all be seen. Open 11:00–20:00 Tuesday–Sunday.

Mani Patam ★★★

Bombay's most revered building can be found at August Kranti gardens, 1km (¾ mile) north of the Walkeshwar/Marine Parade intersection. It was **Mahatma Gandhi's** Bombay home from 1917–1934 and is kept as a shrine to his memory, with his simple *charpoy* (pallet-bed), stick and sandals, and the spinning wheel which Gandhi made into a symbol for India. The telephone by the bed was the Mahatma's sole concession to modern technology. In addition to the plain room in which he worked and lived, there is an extensive library of texts by and about the makers of Indian independence and a small theatre in which films about Gandhi, his political struggles and his ideals are shown. Open 09:30–18:00 Tuesday–Saturday, 09:00–12:00 Mondays.

Hanging Gardens (Ferozeshah Mehta Gardens) ★

Crowning **Malabar Hill**, the Hanging Gardens climb in tiers above Bombay's water reservoirs. In most Indian cities, public green spaces are given exaggerated reverence and are often less exciting to the European than to the local eye. This garden is no exception. The complicated topiary which adorns these gardens is lovely, however, and well worth a look. The hedges and bushes have been cleverly trimmed into the shapes of elephants, tigers, and other beasts. In addition to this, you'll have a wonderful view of Back Bay and the city from the park.

Hidden away behind a nearby wall are the **Towers of Silence**, where Bombay's Parsi community leaves its dead to be eaten by carrion-birds. The site is closed to non-Parsis.

BOMBAY BEACHES

Juhu, 20km (12½ miles) north of central Bombay and close to Santa Cruz airport, is Bombay's beach suburb, with a number of large hotels. It gets crowded at weekends, and the sand is far from pristine and the water is polluted. **Marve**, on the same coast but a further 20km (12½ miles) north, is less built-up. Take note: Bombay's beaches are unsafe for swimmers during the monsoon season.

Above: *The splendid Prince of Wales Museum is a fine example of Indo-Saracenic architecture and houses a marvellous collection of Indian Art.*

DABBA LUNCHES

Bombay has more than 2000 *dabbawallas* – members of a select guild of lunch porters who every day collect more than 100,000 home-made packed lunches from the homes of the city's office workers and deliver them across the sprawling city. Most of the *dabbawallas* are illiterate, but an arcane coding system of coloured symbols guides each meal to the right office desk. Each dabbawalla carries up to 40 of the metal pails called 'tif-fin tins' on a long, narrow wooden tray, racing on foot through Bombay's crowds and traffic. It is claimed that fewer than 20 tins go missing on an average day.

FORT BOMBAY AND COLABA

The oldest part of Bombay, south of Mahatma Gandhi Road and Churchgate and Victoria railway stations, is still called Fort Bombay though there is no longer any trace of the original Portuguese and British fortifications.

Prince of Wales Museum ★★★

Allow at least three hours to view this splendid museum, which has one of the finest collections of Indian art in the world and is an architectural gem in itself. Built in 1905 to mark the visit of the Prince of Wales (later King George V), the museum is in the Indo-Saracenic style, an elegant British pastiche of the architecture of the medieval Mughals. For those who have limited time the key gallery on the ground floor provides an overview of more than 4000 years of Indian art, from clay figurines of the earliest Indus Valley civilization to delightful paintings from the 17th century heyday of the Mughal Empire. If you have plenty of time, you can browse through galleries of statues, secular and temple art, jewellery and archaeological finds, silver and jade, from all over the subcontinent.

If the wildlife reserves of Goa or Kerala are in your schedule, take a look at the museum's natural history section. Open 10:00–17:30 Tuesday–Sunday.

Jehangir Art Gallery ★★★

In the landscaped grounds of the Prince of Wales Museum, the Jehangir Art Gallery houses India's biggest modern art collection, with up to four exhibitions by contemporary Indian painters. The museum is worth a visit mainly for the contrast between old and new artists, but few of the moderns can really compare with the works of the older masters. Open Tuesday–Sunday 10:00–17:30.

Gateway of India ★★★

King George V made his imperial entry to India in 1911 through a temporary structure where this splendid stone arch was erected in 1923. Designed by George Willet,
architect of the Prince of Wales Museum, the 26m (79ft) gateway has four arches and
is another triumph of British-Indian pomp. The statue next to it is of **Shivaji**, the great
16th-century leader of the warlike Maratha people of Maharashtra, who successfully
resisted conquest by the Mughals.

ELEPHANTA ISLAND

Elephanta Island, the only one of the original islands to
have escaped being absorbed into the city sprawl, is
about an hour away by boat from the landing stages
beside the Gateway of India. The trip itself is a welcome
escape from the heat, grime and bustle of downtown
Bombay and the island's main attraction – the **Elephanta
Caves** – is well worth the journey.

The four temples cut into the rock of the island date
from the mid-5th to the mid-8th century AD. The main
cave, which is reached by 125 shallow steps, is finely
decorated to a height of almost 8m (25ft) with intricate
friezework and powerful, fluid frescoes of Shiva in his
creative and destructive aspects. Sadly, many of these
were damaged by the blasphemous Portuguese, who set
up a gun battery on the island and used the temple
decorations as targets.

> **JAINS**
>
> Jainism is among India's
> smaller religions, with fewer
> than four million adherents.
> Like Buddhists, Jains are
> pacifists, adhering to the
> principle of *ahimsa* – respect
> for all forms of life – and
> refusing to harm even
> insects. The sect was found-
> ed about 2500 years ago by
> the Jain teacher, Mahavira.

> **BOMBAY SLUMS**
>
> Bombay's towering apart-
> ment, office and hotel blocks
> are in stark contrast to the
> poverty of its slums.
> People from the villages of
> Maharashtra and neighbour-
> ing states flock to wealthy
> Bombay in search of work.
> Many of them live in squalid
> conditions in shanty-towns
> like **Dharavi**, where more
> than 300,000 people are
> packed into an area of less
> than 200ha (500 acres).

Left: *Rock temples
on Elephanta Island, an
hour away from Bombay,
date from as early as the
5th century.*

Bombay at a Glance

BEST TIMES TO VISIT

Some might argue that there is no good time to visit Bombay. The city is hot all year round, but the 'coolest' months are from **December–March**, when rainfall is minimal and the maximum daytime temperatures are around 30°C (86°F). Avoid the hot, dry months of April and May, as well as the monsoon months of June to mid-October. Rainfall is the heaviest in June and July.

GETTING THERE

Bombay International Airport (Santa Cruz) is some 26km (15 miles) north of the city centre. **Airport buses** operate between Terminal 1 (domestic flights) and Terminal 2 (international flights) and the Air India city terminal at Nariman Point. A police-controlled **taxi** rank operates from both arrival halls. Major downtown hotels also offer a **limousine** service to and from the airport. There is no rail service to the airport from the city centre. Bombay has two long-distance railway stations. Beware confusion: Central Trains go not from the Central Station but from the Victoria Terminus, close to the Fort area of town, which handles trains to Karnataka, Maharashtra and onward connections to Goa, as well as services to Madhya Pradesh, Uttar Pradesh,

Haryana, and Rajasthan. Central Station, north of the city centre, takes care of Western Railway services to Agra and New Delhi, Rajasthan and Gujarat. A **ferry** service also operates between Bombay and Goa six times a week. Tickets and reservations from the MTDC (*see* Useful Contacts).

GETTING AROUND

Self-drive **car rental** is not available in India at present. Cars with a driver can be rented from major hotels, tour and travel agencies. **Taxis** are the best value for money transport option. Virtually all are Indian-built Ambassadors and are not air-conditioned. All are metered, though late at night, drivers are reluctant to switch the meter on and you will have to haggle. **Auto-rickshaws** are found all over India. These three-wheeled scooters with a canopy and bench seat behind the driver are noisy, shaky and open to dust and exhaust fumes but are cheaper and even more plentiful than taxis. They are not metered, and fares must be agreed at the start of your journey. Drivers rarely speak English well and perceive foreigners as soft targets for jacked-up fares. Bargain hard. Bombay has an extensive **bus** network, with London-style double-decker buses. Fares

are very cheap, but avoid the morning and evening rush hours when public transport is very crowded. Buses are not air-conditioned. A suburban electric **rail** network connects central Bombay with its suburbs. The line between Churchgate and Central railway stations takes you through the city centre, with several intermediary stops.

WHERE TO STAY

Bombay offers the range of accommodation you would expect in one of Asia's major business cities. The better hotels cluster around **Nariman Point**, at the south end of **Marine Parade** and overlooking **Back Bay**.

LUXURY

Oberoi Towers, Nariman Point, Bombay 400021, tel: (022) 202 4343. Undoubtedly the best hotel in Bombay's best location.
The Oberoi, Nariman Point, 400021, tel: (022) 202 5757. Slightly more affordable than its sister and almost as palatial.
Taj Mahal Intercontinental, Apollo Bunder, Bombay 400039, tel: (022) 202 3366 International standard hotel near the Gateway of India. Top hotel in Bombay.
Hotel Nataraj, 135 Netaji Subhash Road, Bombay 400020, tel: (022) 204 4161 Upmarket property on Marine Drive. Fine views of the bay.

Bombay at a Glance

Leela Penta Kempinski, Bombay 400059, tel: (022) 636 3636. By far the best hotel near Santa Cruz airport.

MID-RANGE

Ramada Inn Palm Grove, Juhu Beach, Juhu, Bombay 400049, tel: (022) 614 9361 or 614 9343, fax: (022) 614 2105. New member of US chain with a lovely view of Bombay's up-market suburban beach.

Holiday Inn Bombay, Balraj Sahani Marg, Juhu, Bombay 400049, tel: (022) 620 4444. Another new beach suburb hotel in a fashionable area.

Centaur Hotel, Bombay Airport, Bombay 400099, tel: (022) 612 6660. Average, convenient mid-market hotel.

BUDGET

Cheap accommodation is to be found to the south and east of the city centre, in the Colaba Causeway area.

WHERE TO EAT

The best-value restaurants in Bombay – and the most reliable – are those in the city's larger hotels, most of which offer a choice of several types of Indian cuisine as well as European/international and Japanese or Chinese restaurants. Particularly recommended for good food are the restaurants of the **Taj Intercontinental** and both **Oberoi** hotels. (*See* Where to Stay).

SHOPPING

Shopping in Bombay is interesting, with lots of **antique** and **craft** shops selling items from Maharashtra and from all over India. Silk sari lengths are beautiful and inexpensive. Other popular buys are modern and antique paintings and carvings, beautiful silver jewellery from Rajasthan, carved and inlaid wooden boxes, chests and furniture. Fierce bargaining is the norm virtually everywhere. There are **souvenir** and **craft** stores in most large hotels, charging a high premium for run-of-the-mill goods which you could buy much more cheaply elsewhere. Bombay shopkeepers are experts at high-pressure salesmanship; if you feel uncertain about this, and about bargaining, the best choice is the government-operated **Central Cottage Industries Emporium** at 34 Chatrapati Shivaji Maharaj Road, close to the Gateway of India, which sells a glorious assortment of handmade fabrics, furniture, kitchenware, carpets, embroidery, scarves, saris and jewellery.

Shops are open between 10:00 and 19:00, bazaar stalls from 10:00 until around 21:00.

TOURS AND EXCURSIONS

Maharashtra Tourism Development Corporation, CD Hutments, Madame Cama Road, tel: (022) 202 6713 or 202 7762, operates a wide range of excursions around Bombay and throughout Maharashtra state. Destinations include the Ellora and Ajanta cave temples (*see* p.119–120). Information and bookings for state-run hotels, excursions and bus routes across Maharashtra state.

USEFUL CONTACTS

India Tourist Development Corporation, 123 Maharishi Karve Road, Bombay (opposite Churchgate railway station), tel: (022) 291585. Open 08:30–18:00 Monday – Friday, 08:30–13:30 alternate Saturdays. Large collection of free information leaflets and maps on Bombay and India. There are also ITDC information counters at the international airport.

BOMBAY	J	F	M	A	M	J	J	A	S	O	N	D
AVERAGE TEMP. °C	24	25	27	28	30	29	27	27	27	28	27	26
AVERAGE TEMP. °F	75	77	81	82	86	84	81	81	81	82	81	79
HOURS OF SUN DAILY	12	12	12	12	8	4	3	4	6	8	10	12
DAYS OF RAINFALL	1	1	1	1	5	30	30	30	20	10	5	1
RAINFALL mm	2	1	1	3	16	520	710	439	297	88	21	2
RAINFALL in	.1	-	-	.1	.5	20	28	18	12	3.5	.9	.1

3
Panaji and Central Goa

Tiswadi province lies between the **Mandovi** and **Zuari** rivers, tapering towards the narrow western point of Cabo Raj Bhavan. **Panaji** (formerly Panjim), Goa's state capital, lies on the south bank of the broad Mandovi estuary, which broadens to the west into Aguada Bay and the Arabian Sea. Cabo Raj Bhavan separates this bay from the estuary of the Zuari, to the south. Upriver from Panaji lie two river-islands: **Divar**, a genuine island with water on all sides, and **Chorao**, which is in fact a peninsula stretching southwest into the Mandovi from the inland province of Bicholim.

Upriver, too, is **Old Goa**, the long-abandoned Portuguese capital, some 9km (5½ miles) from Panaji. With its ghostly ruined cathedrals on the banks of the Mandovi, this is Goa's most important historic sight and has the biggest concentration of colonial domestic architecture. This colonial capital once stretched all the way between the Mandovi and the Zuari, where the confusingly named present-day village of Goa Velha now stands.

South of the Zuari estuary the narrow peninsula of **Marmagao** juts west into the Arabian Sea. At the tip of this peninsula is Marmagao harbour, a rather grimy industrial seaport. The airport at nearby Dabolim provides most visitors with their first glimpse of Goa. On the south coast of the peninsula, **Bogmalo** beach is fairly small, handy for the airport, and relatively upmarket. Upriver, the Zuari separates Marmagao from **Ponda** province, where a number of striking Hindu temples cluster around the market town of Ponda.

DON'T MISS

*** Church of Our Lady of the Immaculate Conception: this splendid white 17th-century church is Panaji's most striking sight.
*** Old Goa: remnants of the old Portuguese capital, now abandoned, include mighty churches and triumphal arches.
** Dona Paula Beach: the best beach close to Panaji.
** Bogmalo: surprisingly uncrowded beach close to Dabolim Airport.

Opposite: *The Church of St Francis is the best preserved in Old Goa.*

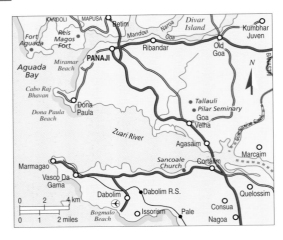

PANAJI

Goa's small capital is, surprisingly, relatively free of tourists. It has its own beaches within easy reach, but they are not the best in Goa and most tourists prefer the purpose-built beach resorts of north and south Goa. Though a state capital, Panaji is no metropolis; much of the time it seems to have more in common with a Portuguese market town than with the throbbing urban sprawl of a typical Indian city. You can walk across it in half an hour, and its major sights can be seen during a leisurely morning's shopping and sightseeing. The best time to visit Panaji is first thing in the morning, when the markets are at their liveliest and the sun is not too hot for strolling. The town goes into siesta mode from early afternoon until dusk when things liven up again.

STATE OF GOA

With a population of about 1.2 million and a land area of only 3702km² (1428 sq miles), Goa is India's smallest state. Though churches are to be seen everywhere, less than 40% of the state's population is Christian, while almost 60% is Hindu. Fishing is an important export industry, with canned and frozen fish being exported mainly to the Far East. Rice is the state's largest crop, with coconut and cashew close behind. The state is also a major producer and exporter of iron ore and bauxite from strip mines in the Bicholim area.

Fontainhas District ★★

Ourem Creek, a tributary of the Mandovi, forms central Panaji's eastern boundary. Fontainhas, the old Portuguese quarter immediately west of the creek, is the most pleasant part of town and is made up of three parallel streets which are connected by narrow lanes. Most of the houses here date from the early 19th century, and although the waterfront has lost its charm with the construction of shabby modern buildings, the rest of the district retains its old-fashioned appeal.

Our Lady of the Immaculate Conception ★★★

The dramatic façade of this Catholic Church, with its elaborate white stucco bell-tower, is the most striking sight in Panaji. The church dominates the **Altinho quarter**, which lies between Fontainhas and the Mandovi waterfront. The first church on the site was built during the earliest years of the Portuguese occupation. It was demolished in 1619 to make way for the present building, which was repeatedly added to and extended throughout the period of Portuguese rule. The most conspicuous addition is the double processional staircase, added in 1871.

Chapel of St Sebastian *

This small chapel in the Fontainhas district was built in 1888. It houses the crucifix from the headquarters of the **Inquisition** in Old Goa which was transferred here after the original capital was finally abandoned by the Portuguese during the 19th century.

Government Secretariat (Sultan's Palace) *

The former palace of Yusuf Adil Shah, Sultan of Bijapur and last Muslim ruler of Goa, is a stately arcaded building on the Mandovi waterfront, much altered since the Portuguese took it over. There is no trace of its original fortifications which guarded the approach from the sea.

Municipal Market *

Goa's covered municipal market stretches several blocks inland from the waterfront and spills out into surrounding streets and alleys. Stalls sell a bewildering array of fresh produce, dried fish, household wares, herbs and spices. This is, however, a market for the local people, so not much of the merchandise is aimed specifically at the tourist, but there is plenty to see and buy on the stalls.

Below: *The Church of Our Lady of the Immaculate Conception dominates Panaji's Altinho quarter.*

Right: *Goan waters are crystal-clear for much of the year but can be muddy during the rainy season.*

GOA'S MUSLIM ERA

Present-day Old Goa was not the first city to be built on this easily defended site with its fine natural harbour. The Kadamba ruler **Jayakeshi I** founded a city called Govapuri near Goa Velha, in the first half of the 11th century. It remained the Kadamba capital until 1343, when it was conquered by the Muslim Sultan, **Jamal ud-Din**. The Kadamba reconquered the city the following year. Some time between 1345 and 1358 it was conquered by the Bahmani Muslims, who in turn lost it to the Hindu king of Vijayanagar. Gopakkapattana survived until 1469, when it was razed to the ground by yet another Bahmani army. The Bahmani conquerors set up their new capital at Ela, where Old Goa now stands, and it was this city that the **Portuguese** took over and expanded. The only surviving trace of the Muslim era is the gate of the Adil Shah's palace.

BEACHES NEAR PANAJI
Miramar *

Panaji's nearest beach is only 3km (2 miles) west of the city, stretching towards Cabo Raj Bhavan. Its rather grubby sands are a popular escape for local people who use it as an impromptu sports ground and meeting place but the water is too muddy and the beach too littered to make swimming or sunbathing attractive propositions.

Dona Paula **

This beach on the south side of the Cabo Raj Bhavan headland and 8km (5 miles) from Panaji is a much more attractive stretch of sand. It is overlooked by the land-scaped grounds and low buildings of the luxury, Moorish casbah-inspired Cidade de Goa hotel. Water-skiing and other watersports are available.

OLD GOA

Old Goa, 9km (6 miles) east of Panaji, is Goa's most outstanding sight. On the banks of the **Mandovi** stands a centuries-old complex of mighty churches, monasteries and convents – all that remains of the once-mighty colonial capital which controlled the trade of Portugal's far-flung overseas empire.

Goa's population was reduced by a series of plagues, and the city was gradually abandoned over a period of three centuries. The disued buildings were demolished and the materials used elsewhere. By the early 19th century only the great places of worship were left to mark the site of the city. Even their days were numbered. In 1835 the Portuguese government disestablished the great church orders and most of Goa's religious community scattered, leaving many of the churches to fall into ruin.

The heart of Old Goa is a complex of three adjoining buildings – the **Se Cathedral**, the **Church of St Francis of Assisi**, and the **Archaeological Museum**, formerly the Convent of St Francis. They are set among tidily kept lawns. A statue of the great Portuguese poet and soldier, Luiz Vaz de Camoes, stands guard over the approach road.

Se Cathedral ***

Commissioned by the Dominican order in 1562, the Se Cathedral was intended to be the greatest church in Portugal's string of Asian colonies. It was not completed until the mid-17th century. Only one of the twin towers survives. The grandiose interior is barrel-vaulted and painted a luminous white, with a magnificent gold altar-piece shows scenes from the life of St Catherine of Alexandria, to whom the cathedral is dedicated.

Above: *Floral decoration on the door of the Basilica of Bom Jesus.*
Below: *The Se Cathedral in Old Goa dates from 1562, the earliest era of the Portuguese conquest.*

VISITING OLD GOA

Allow at least half a day if you plan to visit all the main buildings in Old Goa. The churches, convents and cathedrals cover a considerable area, though no single building justifies a visit of more than about half an hour. Admission to all, including the Museum, was free at the time of writing. There are refreshment stands selling cold bottled drinks at the coach park on the main road and a small open-air café selling drinks and snacks in the grounds of the Se Cathedral.

Above: *Not many of the wooden carvings of saints and the Virgin which once adorned the historic churches have survived.*
Below: *The interior of the Church of St Francis of Assisi is elaborately decorated with scenes from the saint's life.*

LUIS DE CAMOES

Luis de Camoes, whose statue stands in the grounds of the Se Cathedral, arrived in Goa in 1554 as an itinerant soldier and served under the Viceroys of Goa for 16 years, fighting on the Malabar (now Kerala) coast, in Malacca and in Indo-China. During these years he composed his epic poem cycle, *Os Lusiadas*, the greatest work of Portuguese literature. Although the Portuguese erected the statue here in his honour, his work hardly mentions Goa.

Church of St Francis of Assisi *

This is the best-preserved of all Old Goa's great churches. The façade of the church, built in 1661, is three-tiered, with an eight-sided tower on each side. The main entrance is decorated with circular pilasters and a band of rosettes and is the only remaining link to the original building, dating from 1521. It is also the only surviving piece in Asia of the characteristic Manueline church design of 16th-century Portugal. Inside, the nave is barrel-vaulted and the choir is supported by a rib-vaulted crossing. The internal buttress walls are frescoed with floral designs. Above the tabernacle is a large statue of St Francis with Christ on the Cross. Below are statues of St Peter and St Paul. Painted panels on the walls of the nave show scenes from the life of St Francis. Much of the original interior was heavily gilded and painted, and enough remains of it to give some inkling of its glory.

Old Goa Archaeological Museum **

The museum is in the former **Convent of St Francis of Assisi**, between the **Church of St Francis** and the **Se Cathedral**. Its collection is a good guide to the history of Goa before and during the Portuguese period. There are a number of stone slabs and statues from the era of Hindu rule, paintings of Vasco da Gama, Afonso de Albuquerque and later Portuguese grandees, and a collection of coins minted by Portuguese, Muslim, and

Hindu rulers of Goa. Among the most striking exhibits is a stone carving of Vishnu, his consort Lakshmi and his mount, the half-man, half-bird Garuda. Open 10:00–17:00 except Fridays and holidays.

Basilica of Bom Jesus ★★

Opposite the Se Cathedral complex, the basilica church of Good Jesus, built by the Jesuits and consecrated in 1605, is a mixture of lavish gilt and silver with fading paint and crumbling plaster. Outside, exposed red laterite blocks, once stuccoed, and huge buttresses lend an impression of massive solidity. The Baroque west front is its most striking feature. Within, the tomb of **St Francis Xavier** is Goa's holiest relic. Elaborately carved in jasper and decorated by fine bronze plaques depicting scenes from the saint's life, it was given to the church by the Duke of Tuscany, in 1698. The saint lies in a battered solid silver casket.

Above: *Behind the elaborate Baroque façade of the Basilica of Bom Jesus lies the tomb of St Francis Xavier.*

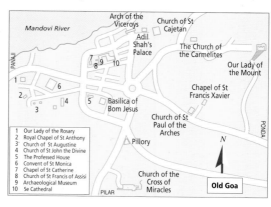

1 Our Lady of the Rosary
2 Royal Chapel of St Anthony
3' Church of St Augustine
4 Church of St John the Divine
5 The Professed House
6 Convent of St Monica
7 Chapel of St Catherine
8 Church of St Francis of Assisi
9 Archaeological Museum
10 Se Cathedral

Above: *Cool, white colonnades surround the inner courtyard of the Professed House.*
Opposite: *A handful of gracious old Portuguese colonial mansions can be seen along Panaji's river front.*

The Professed House *

The Professed House which is the home of the Jesuit order, is cool and quiet. In a corner of the deserted second-floor gallery stands a wooden effigy of a saint, minus its head and which is gradually being eroded by woodworm. The building is still used by the order as a seminary.

Chapel of St Catherine **

This is Old Goa's newest and oldest church. The first chapel was founded by **Afonso de Albuquerque** in 1510. After many additions and subsequent enlargements, the building was completely rebuilt in 1952.

Convent of St Monica **

The convent complex was built in 1637–45 on the site of an earlier convent which was destroyed by fire in 1636. One of the most imposing buildings in Old Goa, it is surprisingly plain inside. Built on a square plan around a central courtyard, the three-storey structure is supported by substantial buttresses both inside and out. The building is now the home of the **Mater Dei Institute**, set up to encourage the study of theology by nuns.

Church and Convent of St John the Divine *

Close to the Convent of St Monica in the section of Old Goa called the **Holy Hill**, the Convent of St John was one of the religious foundations abandoned in 1835 and later passed into the hands of the Convent of St Monica. It was built in 1685 and restored by the Portuguese government in 1961. It is now a Franciscan nunnery.

Church of Our Lady of the Rosary *

This is the oldest church in Old Goa to remain intact. From this spot Albuquerque commanded his troops in the crucial battle for Goa in 1510, and in gratitude for victory built a church which was replaced by the present one in 1549. The church is open only on feast days.

Church of St Cajetan ★★★

Built in 1656–61, this large church's façade is based on the original design of **St Peter's** in Rome. The interior is domed and embellished by seven gilt altarpieces. The church is still in use as a religious college, and following several restorations the building is one of the best preserved of Goa's great religious foundations. Rich wooden carvings on the altar and pulpit are particularly attractive. In the centre of the church is a well which is sometimes claimed to be evidence that St Cajetan's stands on the site of an earlier Hindu temple.

> **ROYAL CHAPEL OF ST ANTHONY**
>
> The Chapel of St Anthony in Old Goa is often called the Royal Chapel. As the patron saint of Portugal, St Anthony was highly regarded. His statue held the rank of captain, and on St Anthony's Day each year the statue was paraded to the colonial treasury to receive its salary, which went into the coffers of the Augustinian order.

Church of St Augustine ★

Two walls of a massive 46m (150ft) belfry mark the colossal wreck of the Church of St Augustine which was built in 1602 and is now reduced to a maze of shattered black laterite walls around a flagged floor set with 17th-century Portuguese tombstones.

Royal Chapel of St Anthony ★

This small chapel next to the ruined Church of St Augustine was dedicated to Portugal's patron saint and built in the early 16th century. Like its neighbour, it was controlled by the **Augustinian** order and abandoned when the order was dissolved in Portuguese lands in 1835. The building was restored in 1894 and again, like several other buildings on the site, in 1961. Next to the shell of ruined St Augustine's it looks almost brand new.

Arch of the Viceroys ★★

The triumphal arch astride the road leading to the Mandovi waterfront is a 1954 restoration of the original arch, which fell down in 1948. The road which passed through the arch was Goa's main thoroughfare, with the **Viceregal Palace** to its left. The original arch was commissioned in 1599 by Francisco da Gama, grandson of the great navigator and governor of Goa in the late 16th century. It was originally a ceremonial entrance to the city from the main anchorage on the Mandovi, and the side facing the river is therefore the most striking. The statue of **Vasco da Gama** which stands within the arch is a clumsy modern replacement of the 16th-century original. The deer carved into the laterite stonework are a memento of his coat of arms.

Gate of the Adil Shah's Palace ★

In front of St Cajetan's Church, a flight of six stone steps leads to a rectangular, decorated stone gateway, the only surviving remnant of the **Palace of the Adil Shah** of Bijapur who ruled the area before the coming of the Portuguese. After the Portuguese conquest, the palace was taken over as the Viceregal residence. When the Viceroys moved their seat from fever-stricken Old Goa, the palace was demolished and its timber and building stone used to build a new one at Panaji. The archway shows signs of Hindu workmanship and was probably looted from a Hindu temple by the Muslim builders.

Below: *The gate of the Adil Shah's Palace is the only remnant of the Muslim dynasty who ruled in Old Goa.*

Church of St Paul of the Arches ★

All that survives of this 16th century church is the stone arch of its main door. It was part of the **College of St Paul**, founded to train Hindu converts as Christian preachers, and was one of the first of Old Goa's churches to fall victim to the city's many epidemics. Consecrated in 1543, it was abandoned in 1570 and left to crumble until the 1830s, when it was demolished for building material. The nearby **Chapel of St Francis Xavier**, where the missionary saint is said to have prayed during his sojourn in Goa, was restored from its ruined state in 1884.

Left: *Glowing stained glass windows illuminate the interior of the Pilar Seminary.*

GOA VELHA AND SURROUNDS

Do not confuse this village, with its scattering of Portuguese-era religious buildings, with Old Goa. Goa Velha, about 16km (10 miles) southeast of Panaji, is on the southern edge of what was once the great colonial city between the Zuari and Mandovi rivers, while Old Goa is some 12km (7½ miles) to the north. Hardly any traces of the old city remain, but there are a couple of sights worth seeing near the present-day village which still bears the old Portuguese name of Goa Velha.

Pilar Seminary ★

The seminary complex north of Goa Velha was founded as a **Capuchin** convent in 1613, abandoned in 1835 and restored by the **Carmelite** order in 1858. It is now in the hands of the **St Francis Xavier Missionary Society**. Its most attractive building is the monastic church, with its magnificent Baroque doorway. The seminary stands on a low hill, and is worth a visit not just in its own right but also for the view of the Zuari and of the site of the former Old Goa inland.

> **PLACENAMES**
>
> Goan placenames and maps can be confusing. There are frequently two or more variations of each name in use, one dating from Portuguese days and one or more recent ethnic versions. Don't confuse the historic site of Old Goa with Goa Velha, several kilometres south. Be careful, too, not to mix up the resorts of Candolim (Kandoli) in northern Goa with Cansaulim in the south. Be aware that Bicholim and Dicholi are the same place, and that Mapusa in the north is also called Mapuca.

Above: *Sweets and fresh fruit juices on sale at a mobile refreshment stall, Vasco da Gama.*

Church of St Anna ★

The Church of St Anna, about 3km (2 miles) north of Goa Velha in the hamlet of **Tallauli** (Talaulim), is one of the grandest religious buildings outside the precincts of Old Goa. Its five-storey façade is unkempt, but the interior is gracefully vaulted, whitewashed and cool. The church was consecrated in 1695, replacing an earlier building dating from the 16th century. It is unlikely to be open except on Sundays and on feast days.

MARMAGAO PROVINCE
Vasco da Gama ★

Named after the famous Portuguese navigator and known universally as just Vasco, this small, busy commercial centre is everything Panaji isn't. It is dominated by freight and import-export businesses, with no historic buildings or sights of interest. The arrival of express trains from out of state adds a brief flurry of excitement several times a day. **Vasco** is of interest only as a transport terminus for those arriving or leaving Goa by rail or looking for bus transport to the southern provinces of Goa or points south.

Marmagao *

This is one of the best natural harbours on India's west coast, rivalled only by Bombay and by Kochi in Kerala. Under Portuguese rule it was of little importance, but since union with India it has become Goa's most important seaport and is also used by the Indian Navy. Many tours of southern and central Goa include a brief stop at Marmagao or a visit to its seaport, through which millions of tons of iron ore are exported each year, and which is one of western India's biggest oil refineries. Many visitors may be surprised to find these included in their itinerary, but India still takes considerable pride in such symbols of progress and industrial development. A passenger ferry service across the mouth of the Zuari connects Marmagao with Dona Paula, on the north shore.

TAXI TIPS

If you are travelling on a package holiday a coach and tour operator representative will be waiting to meet you at Dabolim airport. Independent travellers should head for the official taxi desk, where you pay in advance and are given a slip of paper to hand to your driver. If you are on a tight budget, take a taxi to Vasco da Gama, 5km (3 miles) from the airport, where you can connect with bus and rail services.

Bogmalo **

This beach, only 3km (2 miles) south of Dabolim airport, was naturally one of the first in Goa to be developed for tourism. It is dominated by Goa's first and most obtrusive luxury hotel at its southern end and surrounded by a gaggle of beachside restaurants, bars and souvenir stores along the sandy crescent of beach. Comparatively small by Goan standards – a mere 1km (600 yds) from end to end – Bogmalo, despite its restricted size and the presence of the large hotel complex, does not feel unduly overdeveloped. The beach is a favourite for day visitors from Vasco da Gama and is also conveniently close to Panaji.

Below: *Close to Dabolim Airport, Bogmalo beach is a perfect crescent of white sand and turquoise water.*

Panaji and Central Goa at a Glance

BEST TIMES TO VISIT

The coolest months are from **December** to **March**. The hottest, driest months are during April and May. June and July should be avoided. The later monsoon months of **August** and **September**, are better because this is when the rains slacken and the land is verdant. This can be a delightful time to visit.

GETTING THERE

Goa International Airport is at Dabolim, 30km (19 miles) from Panaji. The drive takes about 45 minutes. The nearest public transport is at Vasco da Gama. Tour buses and tour company couriers meet all charter flight passengers. A well-organized taxi service operates from the airport to points throughout Goa.
Trains to southern Goa and Karnataka leave from Vasco da Gama station. A new railway, the Konkan line, is scheduled to open soon, connecting Vasco and other Goan stations with Maharashtra to the north and coastal Karnataka to the south. Until then, the only ways of getting to Goa from Bombay by train are via Londa and Miraj, a journey of about 21 hours. There are direct services to Bangalore, taking about 20 hours.
Buses for southern Goa also leave from Vasco da Gama. Buses to and from northern Goa leave from the Pato bus

terminal, east of Panaji town centre. Interstate bus travel is not recommended.
A **ferry service** also operates between Bombay and Goa six times a week. Tickets and bookings can be obtained from the **Goa Tourist Development Corporation.**

GETTING AROUND

Cars with a driver can be hired from a number of local and international car hire companies, hotels, and from the Goa Department of Tourism. Self-drive hire is not available.
Taxis can be chartered by the day to explore the region and other parts of Goa, either by negotiating a price with the driver directly or, more easily and usually no more expensively, through a hotel or tour agency. Tourist taxis, usually cream or white, are booked by the journey or by the hour or day through your hotel. Black and yellow ordinary taxis are officially metered, though persuading the driver to use the meter is difficult. Agree a fare before boarding if possible. **Autorickshaws**, three wheeled scooters with a covered bench seat behind the driver, are more expensive than taxis and are used only for short hops. Public **buses** are frequent but quite slow; longer journeys require several changes. Buses are open, so journeys are breezy but dusty. Air-conditioned tour

buses and minibuses can be chartered by groups through local tour agencies. The road journey between Vasco and Panaji involves a long detour to the first bridge across the Zuari. Passenger **ferries** operate between Marmagoa and Dona Paula.

WHERE TO STAY

Panaji offers a range of accommodation including basic backpacker's hotels and a number of mid-range, locally owned properties, but no large international-style resort hotels. There is no accommodation in Old Goa.

LUXURY
Cidade de Goa: Vainguinim Beach, Dona Paula, tel: (022) 0834 53301/12, fax: 43303. Award-winning luxury beach complex overlooking the best beach in the Panaji area.

MID-RANGE
La Paz Gardens Hotel, Swatatraya Path, Vasco da Gama, tel: (022) 2121/26, 2738. Vasco's largest, most expensive modern hotel.
Fidalgo Hotel, 18th June Road, Panaji, tel: (022) 46291/99. Large (129-room) mid-range hotel with a choice of restaurants, swimming pool and gym.
Mandovi Hotel, D. B. Bandodkar Marg, Panaji, tel: (022) 46270/79. Comfortable hotel with 69 rooms.

Panaji and Central Goa at a Glance

Golden Goa Hotel, Dr Atmaram Borker Road, Panaji, tel: (022) 46231/39, fax: 44090. Small (36-room) hotel with good facilities including swimming pool.
Keni's Hotel, 18th June Road, Panaji, tel: (022) 44581/83. Cheaper medium-sized hotel.

BUDGET

Vasco Tourist Hotel, Vasco da Gama, tel: (022) 0834 513119. Government-run hotel. Reasonably priced option for those forced to stay in Vasco to catch an early train or flight.
Panjim Inn, E-212 31st January Road, Fontainhas, Panaji, tel: (022) 226523 or 227169. Pleasant hotel, family run with carved wooden four-poster beds, fans, mosquito nets and there are balconies overlooking the courtyard.

WHERE TO EAT

Note that in Goa, as elsewhere in India, small local restaurants may be called 'hotels' even though they have no bedrooms attached.

Panaji

Goa's capital does not have as many restaurant options as the state's popular beach resorts. For evening meals, the best bet is to head for one of the hotels, which usually offer a range of Goan, Asian and European meals.
Hotel Venite, Post Office Road, Fontainhas. Not a hotel but a delightful old-fashioned restaurant on the first floor, with wrought-iron balconies overlooking the street and polished wooden floors. The most atmospheric place to eat and drink in Panaji.
Fidalgo Hotel, European, Goan and Chinese cuisine.
Mandovi Hotel, Goan, Chinese, Portuguese and European menus.
Keni's Hotel, Indian, Chinese and Goan dishes.
Golden Goa, European, Goan and Chinese cuisine.

Vascoln Vasco

It's best to eat at the restaurants of the La Paz Gardens Hotel, which offers a choice of Indian, Goan, Chinese and European-style cuisine.

Old Goa

A small outdoor café in the grounds of the Se Cathedral sells soft drinks and snacks in the shade of a huge tree. There are also cold drink stands beside the coach park.

Bogmalo

A surprisingly good choice of small seafood restaurants offering excellent value. Most of them cluster beside the semi-permanent market village at the south end of the beach.

SHOPPING

Shopping in Panaji is patchy. The Municipal Market is a great place to browse for less likely souvenirs such as nests of shiny tiffin tins, sandals, cheap glittery jewellery or retro-style Indian luggage. There are several souvenir shops and tailors in the streets nearby. At Bogmalo, there is a thriving, semi-permanent tourist market at the south end of the beach. This comes into its own at dusk, and sells brightly coloured clothes and accessories from all over India. Prices are inflated and bargaining is strongly recommended.

TOURS AND EXCURSIONS

Goa Tourist Development Corporation operates a number of sightseeing tours starting from Panaji and Vasco. These include all-day tours to North and South Goa beaches, tours of the Old Goa churches and the Hindu temples around Ponda, and longer two-day trips to the inland Dudhsagar waterfalls and the Bondla and Bhagwan Mandir wildlife sanctuaries. The GDTC also offers a range of one-hour sunset, sundown, and full moon **cruises**, as well as longer half-day trips on the Mandovi and Zuari rivers.

USEFUL CONTACTS

Government of Goa Tourist Information Office, Tourist Home, Patto, Panaji, tel: (022) 45583, 45715, 44757. Leaflets, maps, list of hotels and guesthouses, bookings for state-run hotels and wildlife reserve bungalows, excursions and ferry bookings.

4
Northern Goa

The **beaches** of northern Goa between the Mandovi River in the south and the Chapora River in the north are the most popular in the state. There are a string of hotels stretching up the coast from the ramparts of the 17th-century Portuguese **Fort Aguada** almost as far as the 18th-century stronghold at **Chapora**, overlooking **Vagator** beach and village. Most of these hotels cater to a mixed British, northern European and Indian clientele. Fort Aguada itself happens to be one of the most expensive hotels in Goa. Most of the beaches along this part of the coast are long stretches of bright golden sand, backed by palms which mask the hotel buildings. Most Goan coastal villages stand some distance from the high water line, helping to preserve the illusion of an untouched tropical paradise. During the monsoon season, between mid-June and the end of August, the beaches are less attractive. Heavy surf removes much of the sand, the small shacks and bars close down, and frequent torrential downpours send people scurrying for cover.

North of the Chapora River, development is far less extensive, and the region's emptier beaches and simple village facilities attract a very different clientele of hard core hippies – many of whom live in Goa for much of the year – and independent travellers taking a break from the long-haul overland trail through Asia. Rocky headlands split by most of the beaches along Goa's far north coast are smaller than those south of the Chapora, with small villages hidden away in the coconut palm gardens inland.

DON'T MISS

*** Fort Aguada: massive medieval bastions enclose five star hotels and a fine secluded beach.
*** Anjuna: fantastic stretch of uncrowded beach, a small, relaxed village and a lively weekly market.
** Chapora: 16th-century hilltop fortress stands on a headland overlooking fine beaches.
** Vagator: uncrowded coves of golden sand.

Opposite: *Fringed with palms, white sands sweep north through Calangute, now a popular resort.*

Fort Aguada ✱✱✱

During the early 17th century, the Portuguese turned this northern headland of the **Mandovi** into a powerful fortress to control the mouth of the river. In 1612 they cut a channel across the neck of the headland between the Mandovi and the smaller **Nerul River** to the north, making Aguada into an artificial island. Throughout the period of Portuguese conquest and consolidation it proved impregnable from both sea and land. From its walls, 79 great guns raked every approach and commanded the entrance to the Mandovi.

Massive laterite walls and bastions surround the island, some of them in good repair, others crumbling into ruin. On the north shore, at the mouth of the Nerul, the battlements overlook a small fishing harbour, while a circular bastion-jetty, jutting out to sea, effectively cuts off the beach immediately in front of the island from the much longer stretch of sand to the north. The outer fortress walls, entered by a bridge across the currently dry moat, now contain several of Goa's top luxury resort complexes, none of them too obtrusive thanks to the surrounding palms and other greenery.

Just inside the main gateway of the citadel is Aguada's most prominent landmark, the squat 13m (42ft) white tower of the **lighthouse** built in 1864. Above it, on the highest point of the headland, is the pretty little church of **St Lawrence**, patron saint of sailors, which was built in 1630.

The main citadel of the fortress also houses guests, but not willing ones. It is used as a **prison**. So is another Portuguese fortress, **Reis Magos**, some 9km (5½ miles) east of Aguada on the north coast of the Mandovi. Next to its grim walls stands the **Church of Reis Magos** (Church of the Magi Kings), built in 1555 and restored during the 18th century. The steps to the church are guarded by carved stone lions, probably looted from an earlier Hindu temple, and the royal coat of arms of Portugal is carved above the door.

BEACH ETIQUETTE

Indian tourists flock to Goa's hippy beaches in the hope of catching a glimpse of naked Western flesh, and it is not unusual to see a respectable Indian trying to persuade a topless western girl to pose with him for a souvenir photo. Though many young visitors wear the absolute minimum on the beach, displays of public nudity are technically illegal and very much frowned on by local people. Modesty is a way of life for Indians of all castes and religions.

FORT AGUADA TO THE CHAPORA

Sinquerim beach sweeps north from Fort Aguada in an unbroken stretch of sand terminating in a rocky headland at the end of **Baga** beach. The villages of **Candolim, Calangute** and **Baga** which are strung out along this beach have grown into popular holiday resorts. The main attraction of each of these is the beach, but a few pretty churches dating from the 17th and 18th century lend some historic and architectural interest to the area. The northern stretch of coast beyond Baga has so far escaped full-scale tourist development. This area was the first of Goa's 1960s hippy havens, but with the growth of more orthodox package tourism the counter-culture has moved on to more remote strands in the far north and deep south.

Below: *Bastions stretch into the sea at Fort Aguada, one of north Goa's most expensive resorts.*

Northern Goa is less well endowed with sights to see than the central provinces. The beach is the main attraction, while inland the countryside is a mixture of seemingly endless paddy fields and coconut groves. Beach life for visitors centres on swimming and sunbathing with few of the powered watersports such as waterskiing or parascending. This is mainly because of the prohibitive cost of importing equipment. Relaxation, however, is what most visitors are after, and relaxation is what this stretch of coast delivers supremely well – whether in the luxury

hotels and package holiday resorts on the southern stretch of the coast or in the simple budget-traveller encampments to the north. A host of informal services have sprung up to make beach life even more relaxing. Fruit vendors bring you slices of pineapple or drinking coconuts, masseurs offer to relieve your aches and pains; cold drink vendors, jewellery pedlars and the occasional furtive marijuana dealer will also stroll by. Beach business is an entertainment in itself.

Candolim (Kandoli) ★★

Not to be confused with Cansaulim in southern Goa, the first resort settlement north of Aguada is situated about 400m (1312ft) inland from the shore. Newer hotel and restaurant buildings surround the mid-17th century **Church of Our Lady of Hope**. The church is typically grandiose, and seems far too large for the tiny fishing and farming village Candolim was before the coming of tourism. Its tall decorative towers – a later 18th-century addition – dominate the village.

WATERSPORTS

Goa's beaches offer a limited choice of watersports, as importing and maintaining powered equipment is quite expensive. **Water-skiing** and **jetskis** are available at major resorts though, including those at Fort Aguada. **Scuba** training and dive trips are also offered at Calangute. Watersports are not available during the monsoon season.

Calangute (Kalangut) *

North of Candolim, Calangute is about 1km (⅔ mile) inland, at the crossroads of the main north–south route and the coastal road to **Baga** and **Calangute** beach. The resort is the biggest and most popular in northern Goa, despite its steeply shelving beach. Much of its sand is stripped away during the monsoon but is gradually being replaced throughout the winter. Watersports are plentiful, as are beach pedlars, who can be irritatingly persistent. The newer holiday village, with its hotels and bars, merges imperceptibly into the older settlement. Like Candolim, Calangute is built around a decorative Portuguese church, dedicated to St Alex and faced by an elaborate artificial grotto.

Saligao *

The village of Saligao, 2km (1¼ miles) east of Calangute, is poised to merge with the larger settlement in the fairly near future, with building already spilling over the coastal highway. Saligao is worth the short detour from Calangute for a look at its lovely, whitepainted **Church of the Rosary**. Built in 1873, it is in a sharp-edged, angular neo-Gothic style which sets it apart from the Baroque or Manueline churches which are more commonly seen in Goa's towns and villages.

Above: *A pagoda-like shrine beside a busy main highway is a reminder that Goa is Hindu as well as Catholic.*
Left: *Church of the Rosary (Church of Our Lady Mother of God) at Saligao with its neo-Gothic tower.*
Opposite: *The Church of Our Lady of Hope, with its twin white towers, is a landmark for the village of Candolim.*

PARTY TIME

Anjuna is famed for its full moon parties, when hundreds of young ravers from all over the world gather to hear the latest in dance music played by DJs from Europe's trendiest nightspots. Each party is an all-night, high-decibel event, and you can find out when and where the next one will be held by asking around in the more relaxed beach bars. If it's too loud, you're too old.

Baga ★★★

This is the northernmost resort village on **Sinquerim** and has the best beach north of Aguada. Baga is sheltered by a headland which cuts it off from the smaller, more intimate beaches of the Anjuna–Vagator area to the north. A mixture of good-value, mid-market hotels and restaurants makes it a popular package holiday resort. However, the flotilla of wooden fishing boats hauled up on the beach or moored offshore is a reminder of the old, traditional way of life of the village. The hotels and restaurants are spread out along the main highway, which runs only 100m (330ft) from the beach. Baga also offers other options: walk south to the bigger choice of restaurants and watersports at **Calangute**, or north over the headland to the less developed beaches of **Anjuna** and **Vagator**.

Anjuna ★★★

Large-scale tourism development comes to an abrupt halt north of the Baga headland, and many people would argue that this is where the 'real' Goa starts. Anjuna village and its sprawling collection of cheap accommodation and eating places are favoured more by backpackers and other independents rather than by the mainstream holiday-makers. Despite the beginnings of more middle-of-the-road development the atmosphere remains very different from that of Baga or Calangute –

reminiscent in fact of a more-or-less continuous alternative lifestyle festival. This is interrupted only by the monsoon, when the counter-culture crowds head back to Europe, Australia or the USA, to return when the rain stops in September. Anjuna comes into its own once a month

for its famous (or notorious) **full moon party**, an institution since the 1970s, when everyone heads for the beach for a night of raving and loud music. If you intend to join the festivities, be aware that the crowd is always infiltrated by plain-clothed Indian policemen keen to improve their arrest record.

Anjuna's other major event is the **weekly fleamarket**, held each Wednesday. You are unlikely to find anything here that you have not been offered in village shops or by beach vendors, but it is a great place to go for a morning's one-stop-shopping for all your holiday souvenirs and gifts. The main stock in trade is brightly coloured garments and glittering jewellery from all over India and – because competition between vendors is intense – you are in a better bargaining position than when you are haggling one-to-one with a beach pedlar.

Vagator **

A track leads over the hill north of Anjuna village to the attractive beaches of Vagator. The two golden sand coves are separated by rugged black reefs. Tiny shacks line the beach, competing to play the latest and loudest dance music day and night on battery-powered sound systems. The clientele is young and on a small budget, and some people camp on the slopes above the beach.

Above: *Brilliantly coloured fabrics and jewellery at Anjuna's weekly flea market are a photographer's delight.*
Opposite: *Anjuna, with its idyllic sandy coves separated by rocky headlands, is where the 'real' Goa begins.*

DRUGS

Goa's beaches have been a byword for soft drugs, mainly **bhang** and **hashish**, since the 1960s. With the growth in mainstream tourism, local authorities have become even keener to prosecute drug users. Drug dealers who approach potential customers on the beach, on the street or in cheap accommodation often double as police informers. Possession of even small amounts is punishable by long prison sentences.

Above: *Fort Chapora's grim battlements stand on a hilltop overlooking one of Goa's most magnificent beaches.*
Opposite: *An onion seller surrounded by mounds of his wares at Mapusa's busy produce market, held every Friday.*

Chapora **

Overlooking the Vagator coves atop a bare hill of black laterite boulders stands the grim-looking **Fort Chapora**. Its ring of ramparts, studded with Portuguese-domed bastions, dates from the 18th century, when the Portuguese built a chain of forts to link and defend their Indian territories. An earlier Muslim fortress, known as **Shapur**, belonged to the Adil Shah, the last Muslim ruler of Goa. There is nothing to see inside the walls other than the bastions on each side which offer fine views south along the sweeping beaches towards Fort Aguada and north over the estuary of the **Chapora River**.

Chapora village is on the south bank of the river, east of the fort and sheltered from the sea by the headland on which the fort stands. A fair-sized fishing fleet anchors in this safe natural harbour, and Chapora is still a fishing village with a little low-budget tourism, not a former village turned full-scale resort.

MAPUSA AND BEYOND THE CHAPORA

Beyond the Chapora River, in **Pernem** province, lies Goa's longest stretch of undeveloped beach, protected from mass tourism by its inaccessibility. Getting there involves a long journey inland to the first crossing of the Chapora at **Colvale**, or a trip on the ferry between Siolim, 5km (3 miles) upriver from Chapora, and **Chordem** on the north bank.

Mapusa *

Some 20km (12½ miles) inland from Chapora, Mapusa is the main town of **Bardez** province and the main transport junction for travel to the Vagator area and points north of the river.

Mapusa Friday Market *

Mapusa is the venue for one of Goa's biggest produce markets. Held each Friday and well worth a visit, it draws buyers and vendors from all over northern and central Goa. The contrast between this busy market selling everyday household goods and all sorts of fruit, vegetables, fish, herbs and spices and the Wednesday market which is geared towards tourists at Anjuna could not be greater. Visit early in the morning to see the thronged market at its liveliest.

Church of Our Lady of Miracles *

Consecrated in 1594, the church has a fine Baroque front which is deceptively modern. It has been rebuilt many times, most recently in 1962 and was built on the site of an earlier Hindu temple. Mapusa is noted for its annual festival of Our Lady of Miracles, celebrated by Hindus and Christians alike on the first Sunday 16 weeks after Easter. Goan Christians hold it in honour of the **Virgin Mary** and Hindus in veneration of their virgin goddess **Lairaya**.

Pernem **

North of Mapusa on the main road, Pernem, is the capital of Pernem province, the northernmost part of Goa and is separated from the neighbouring state of Maharashtra by the Tiracol River. The village has several noteworthy and highly colourful Hindu temples.

> **BARGAINING TIPS**
>
> Hard bargaining is the rule in markets like those at **Mapusa** or on the beach at **Anjuna**. You may find you will be able to negotiate a better bulk price for several items than by negotiating for each purchase separately. At the beach market, you should be able to bring the asking price down by anywhere from 30 to 60%, but at Mapusa don't expect to squeeze more than 10% off.

Shri Baghavati Temple **

The temple to Bhagavati, one of the destructive aspects of Shiva's spouse Parvati, is impossible to miss, located along one side of the main square with lifesize stone elephants guarding its entrance. Within the temple, Bhagavati is represented by a massive statue carved from black basalt.

Mauli Temple *

About 1km (⅔ mile) from Pernem, this small temple
houses a black stone statue of the goddess Mauli and is
prettily located beside the small Sarmal waterfall.

Deshprabhu House **

This rambling Hindu mansion is the most magnificent
family home in Goa. The **Deshprabhu** family were
aristocrats under Portuguese rule, and the grandiose
19th-century building with its 16 inner courts is a token
of their wealth and power. Not all the courtyards are
open to casual visitors. The first courtyard houses a family temple and a small museum with a collection which
gives a fascinating insight into the life of an important
landowning Hindu family. The most striking pieces in
the collection are the solid silver palanquins in which
family retainers carried the Deshprabhu children to the
temple on Hindu festivals. Open 10:00–17:00 except
Fridays and holidays.

Below: *Flimsy outrigger-
style fishing boats like this
one landing its catch at
Arambol are still widely
used in Goa.*

Arambol **

The superb, untouched beach stretches unbroken for
12km (7½ miles) from the mouth of the Chapora as far
as this quintessential Goan fishing village and hippy
hideaway. Arambol village is around 1km (½ mile)

inland. Accommodation and facilities are extremely basic and are likely to remain so until improved access makes Arambol an attractive prospect to the hotel developers.

Above: *Built by the Portuguese, the tiny fort at Tiracol on Goa's northern border is now a comfortable hotel.*

Tiracol ★★
This is Goa's last outpost in the north. A tiny Portuguese **fort** dating from the 18th century when the Portuguese captured an earlier fortress from the local Raja, stands on a hillock guarding the river mouth. Within its ramparts are a small chapel to **St Anthony** and a government-run tourist hotel.

Alorna ★
Some 16km (10 miles) east of the main highway, on the southern tributary of the Chapora River, this small **fort** is one of the few inland strongholds built by the Portuguese. Its purpose was to defend the river crossing against **Maratha** raiders from the north. Apart from the crumbling ramparts there is little to see.

BICHOLIM AND SURROUNDS
Bicholim province lies north of the Mandovi, east of the Mapusa River, and south of the state border with Maharashtra.

MARKETS

Markets like those to be found in most Goan towns are good places to shop for unusual **souvenirs**. Aromatic spices are good additions to your kitchen at home, and the stainless-steel tiffin tins with tight-fitting lids sold on many stalls are attractive storage containers. You can even buy a typical Indian tin suitcase, painted in bright floral patterns, to take your new purchases home in.

Below: *The chapel in Tiracol Fort served local villagers as well as the garrison.*

Bicholim (Dicholi) ★

Bicholim, the small main town of the province, is surrounded by a scattering of Hindu temples. The best way to visit these is with a hired car and a driver who is familiar with the district, as they are not signposted.

Shri Datta Mandir Temple ★

The 19th-century temple on the banks of the Mandovi is of unusual design, with a blue multi-tiered spire instead of the domed roof more common in Goan Hindu temples.

Vithal Mandir Temple ★★

The local god Vithal may date back to Dravidian times. His statue in this small temple is richly dressed, carved of local black laterite, and flanked by images of Lakshmi, consort of Vishnu, and Sarasvati, consort of Brahma.

Lamgao Cave Temples ★

These caves just outside Bicholim village can only be reached on foot. Both are Hindu holy places, the smaller cave containing a phallic lingam altar and a stone carving of the Nandi bull, the steed of Shiva. The caves are believed to have been dug originally by Buddhist monks and worshippers.

Arvalem Caves and Waterfalls ★★

The earliest cave temples in Goa are in a series of rock outcrops southeast of the village of Sanquelim. Excavated some time between the third and the sixth centuries AD, each contains a Shiva lingam. Like those at Lamgao, they were probably the work of local Buddhists. A number of Buddha statues have been discovered in and around the area of Sanquelim village.

Northern Goa at a Glance

BEST TIMES TO VISIT

See p. 54.

GETTING THERE

Fort Aguada and Sinquerim resorts: buses (1–2 hours) depart from Panaji and Mapusa approximately every hour.
Chapora, Vagator and Anjuna: buses (1½ hours) from Panaji to Mapusa. Change buses at Mapusa or take an auto-rickshaw from Mapusa bus station.
Mapusa: Buses (1½ hours) from Panaji.
Pernem: Buses leave from Mapusa. To reach Arambol and the coast of Pernem province, take an auto-rickshaw from Pernem. Also very occasional buses.
Bicholim and surrounds: Buses arrive roughly every three hours from Mapusa.

GETTING AROUND

A pleasant way to visit Anjuna's Wednesday flea market is by **fishing boat** from Baga or Calangute.
Taxis and chauffeur-driven **cars** are available through the hotels in the main resorts.
Auto-rickshaws wait at the bus stations in Mapusa and Bicholim.

WHERE TO STAY

The stretch of coast between Fort Aguada and the Chapora contains Goa's widest range of accommodation. North of the Chapora, in Pernem province, there are no hotels of any kind, and accommodation is in simple beach huts or private homes. Finding a room is a matter of turning up and asking around.

LUXURY
Fort Aguada Beach Resort, Sinquerim, tel: (022) 7501/09. Finest luxury hotel, within the walls of the old fortress.
Taj Holiday Village, Sinquerim, tel: (022) 7501/09. Equally luxurious as the Fort Aguada Beach Resort.

MID-RANGE
Baia do Sol Hotel, Baga Beach, Calangute, tel: (022) 7501/84/85. Small, friendly mid-range hotel on the beach at Baga.
Aldeia Santa Rita, Baga Beach, Calangute. Very attractive village-style resort 200m (656ft) from the beach at Baga. Accommodation in small four-room blocks in old Portuguese mansion style, built around a small pool.
Vagator Beach Resort, Siolim. This is a simply designed, low rise resort with an unbeatable location right on northern Vagator beach, below the fort.

BUDGET
Mapusa Tourist Hotel, Mapusa, tel: (022) 0832 26 27 94 or 26 26 94. Functional government-operated hotel in the centre of Mapusa.

WHERE TO EAT

Sinquerim
There are so many beach restaurants which often change hands from season to season that it is pointless to list them here. Virtually all the small restaurants which cluster around the resorts are friendly and offer good value for money. Use your discretion.

Anjuna
Vast choice of beach restaurants and food stalls.

Chapora
The main street is lined with small open-air restaurants and food stalls.

Mapusa
It is advisable to wait and eat at your resort destination.

Pernem Province Beaches:
The restaurant scene in the northernmost Goa beaches is even more informal than in Anjuna or Chapora.

TOURS AND EXCURSIONS

There is no information currently about tours and excursions in this region. Please see p. 55 and use this as a reference.

USEFUL CONTACTS

There are no tourist or information offices outside Panaji; for information see p. 55, Central Goa and Panaji.

5
Eastern Goa

Ponda, Sanguem and Satari, the landlocked provinces of central and eastern Goa, are often overlooked by visitors whose main focus is on the beaches and the sights of Panaji and Old Goa. Both Ponda and Sanguem offer the visitor different aspects of Goa, away from the holiday hotels and Portuguese churches and cathedrals. Added to the Portuguese empire much later than the coastal provinces, this part of Goa seems much more a part of India. Its landscapes, too, are different and more dramatic, with the forested slopes of the **Western Ghats** mountain range rising away from the coastal plain.

Ponda's attractions are mainly historic and manmade. The province is Goa's Hindu heartland, with the largest concentration of Hindu temples in the state, while on its eastern border the **Bondla Wildlife Sanctuary** offers a glimpse of Goa's wilder side. Ponda borders Tiswadi in the northwest and is separated from Bicholim by the upper reaches of the **Mandovi River**, while the **Upper Zuari River** divides it from Marmagao and Salcete in the west. The easiest way to explore Ponda is with a car and driver hired at your holiday base, but there are also a number of tours which take in the high points of its Hindu temples, with or without a visit to Bondla.

Sanguem province is long and thin, bordering the provinces of Satari to the north and Ponda, Salcete, Quepem and Canacona to the west. To the east, the ranges of the Western Ghats divide it from Karnataka state. Sanguem is tailormade for rail travel, with

DON'T MISS

*** **Ponda:** colourful Hindu temples are scattered around this picturesque region.
*** **Tambdi Surla Temple:** ancient Hindu temple, hidden away among wooded hills.
** **Baghwan Mahavir Wildlife Sanctuary:** offers excellent bird watching and game drives.
** **Dudhsagar Falls:** interesting train ride through spectacular scenery.

Opposite: *The Shri Shantadurga Temple, dating back almost four centuries, shows its Portuguese influences.*

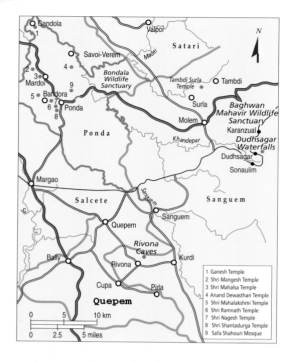

1 Ganesh Temple
2 Shri Mangesh Temple
3 Shri Mahalsa Temple
4 Anand Dewasthan Temple
5 Shri Mahalakshmi Temple
6 Shri Ramnath Temple
7 Shri Nagesh Temple
8 Shri Shantadurga Temple
9 Safa Shahouri Mosque

Goa's main railway line from Vasco da Gama to Karnataka and points east cutting across the province and winding its way through the passes of the Western Ghats to the Karnataka plateau across the state border.

The province's main attractions are natural, and conveniently close to the railway line. They include the impressive **Dudhsagar Falls**, one of India's highest waterfalls. Near the village of **Molem** is the second of Goa's wildlife sanctuaries, and at **Tambdi Surla** one of Goa's oldest Hindu temples survives.

Satari, the third of the inland provinces, borders Bicholim in the west and Sanguem in the south, with the state borders of Maharashtra and Karnataka on its north and east sides. Those keen to get off the beaten track will find that the province has something to offer. Getting to the main town of **Valpoi** will require several bus changes or your own transport.

PONDA

During the first two centuries of the Portuguese conquest, all temples and mosques in Portuguese territory were destroyed. By the time Ponda came under Portuguese rule in 1764 there was greater toleration, and its temples have survived, though almost all have been rebuilt and restored so many times that nothing remains of the original building. Most are within an 8km (5 mile) radius of Ponda village.

Opposite: *Sacred cows wander freely through the Shantadurga Temple grounds while worshippers look on.*

Hindu temples follow the same pattern throughout Goa, and many visitors may feel that a visit to more than one is overdoing it. Frequent restoration, repainting and rebuilding means that, despite their age, they impress the foreigner with little sense of history and none of the grandeur of the echoing, empty and dilapidated Portuguese cathedrals.

Shri Nagesh Temple ★★

This temple, 1km (½ mile) from the village of **Farmagudi** on the main Ponda road, is more brightly coloured than many local shrines, with vividly painted gods and demons around the base of its squat tower. A black stone slab mounted in the wall dates the temple from at least the early 15th century. An effigy of the Nandi bull, the mount of Shiva, stands outside the entrance to the temple hall. Nagesh is an aspect of Shiva, and the temple contains several lingam and mukhalingam shrines.

Shri Shantadurga Temple ★★★

There has been a temple to Shri Shantadurga – an aspect of Parvati – near **Kavalem**, just outside Ponda town, for at least four centuries, but the existing one clearly shows the Portuguese influence which had begun to alter the design of local temples by that time. It is the largest of Ponda's temples and attracts many pilgrims on Hindu holy days. Two towers overlook a huge flagged courtyard. The doors to the shrine are heavily decorated in silver, and within stands a marble statue of Shantadurga accompanied by images of Shiva and Vishnu.

DRIVING IN INDIA

Both chauffeur-driven and self-drive car hire are available from major international chains in India. When driving, bear in mind that roads are often poorly maintained and traffic can be intimidating, with diesel-belching trucks, buses, jeeps and taxis jockeying for position. Hazards unique from India include sacred cows, which hold up traffic and woe betide the driver who collides with one! Roads are also haphazardly signposted so navigation can be a problem. It's better to hire a driver who knows the roads. Chauffeur-driven hire cars are among India's travel bargains.

Above: *The Shri Mangesh temple is Goa's most famous temple and usually the only one visitors will be taken to see.*

Shri Ramnath Temple ★★★

Only 100m (330ft) from the Shri Shantadurga Temple, the Shri Ramnath Temple is dedicated to **Shiva**. Its inner hall is one of the most lavishly decorated in the region, with embossed silver on the wall of the sanctuary and elaborate friezes and reliefs surrounding the entrance arch and supporting columns.

Shri Mahalakshmi Temple ★

This temple near **Bandora**, about 5km (3 miles) from Ponda, is dedicated to **Lakshmi**. Its doors are guarded by an image of Ganesh, and murals of the Garuda bird and the monkey-god Hanuman decorate the doorway. Founded in the early 15th century, it houses an image of Mahalakshmi, the great goddess, spirited away from the Portuguese in 1565.

Shri Mahalsa Temple ★★

This temple close to **Mardol** village on the main Ponda–Old Goa road dates from the 17th century and is noteworthy for the elaborately carved wooden pillars which support its roof. A 21-tiered brass column supporting a tiny effigy of the Garuda bird, the mount of Vishnu, stands in the courtyard, overlooked by a pink and white pagoda-like tower. The temple is sacred to Mahalsa, an incarnation of the goddess Lakshmi.

ANCIENT AND MODERN

Most of Goa's Hindu temples stand on centuries-old sites, but the temples themselves look remarkably modern compared with the crumbling cathedrals of Old Goa. Temples are frequently refurbished, repainted and even completely rebuilt, though they may contain very ancient images of the gods. An exception is the **Shri Mahadeva Temple** at Tambdi Surla, which has been long abandoned.

Shri Mangesh Temple ★★★

This temple at **Priol**, 8km (5 miles) north of Ponda town, is Goa's most impressive Hindu temple, and if you have the time or inclination to visit only one, this should be it. A pagoda-like octagonal lamp-tower, the tallest and most impressive in the state, rises above a pretty, recently restored main building in the typically Goan colours of primrose yellow, white and terracotta. The temple is built around the largest water tank in Goa and is surrounded by greenery and palm trees. Mangesh is a benevolent aspect of Shiva. The temple dates from the 17th–18th centuries.

Ganesh Temple ★

This small temple at **Candola** village, some 24km (15 miles) from Ponda on the banks of the Mandovi River, is dedicated to the elephant-headed god of prosperity and wisdom, Ganesh. Ganesh or Ganapati was the protective god of Ela, the earlier Hindu city on the site of Old Goa, and the older of the two Ganesh statues in this shrine was removed from there after the city fell to Muslim invaders from Bijapur.

Below: *The small but interesting Shri Nagesh temple in Ponda dates from the 18th century. Reliefs of brightly painted gods decorate the lamp tower.*

Below: *One of Goa's few mosques, the Safa Shahouri Masjid, is a survivor from before the Portuguese conquest.*

Anand Dewasthan Temple ★

The Anand Dewasthan Temple, near **Savoi-Verem** village, features on a number of tour itineraries but is perhaps less striking than some of the other shrines of Ponda province, having no multi-tiered tower or domed roof. It is however prettily located in the countryside near the upper Mandovi River.

Safa Shahouri Mosque (Masjid) ★★★

Just outside Ponda, the mosque was built at the command of **Ali Adil Shah**, Sultan of Bijapur, in 1560. It was partially destroyed by the Portuguese, and is one of only two mosques surviving from the Bijapur period. Compared with the nearby Hindu temples it is a plain, restrained building, with Bijapuri-style pointed arches inside and out. The stumps of octagonal pillars that surround it indicate that the pitched roof originally extended to cover the stone platform around the *masjid*. Stone steps lead from the entrance to the large tank on the south side of the building.

Bondla Wildlife Sanctuary ★★

The smallest and most easily accessible of Goa's three wildlife sanctuaries is around 20km (12½ miles) east of Ponda town and is featured on a number of tour itineraries. Visitors expecting a safari-style experience or a trek through virgin forest will be disappointed, as Bondla is a pocket-sized park. Its main attraction is a series of zoo-style enclosures. Species on show include **leopard**, **sambar deer** and **gaur**. A walk in the beautifully landscaped

Above: *Peacocks run wild in the grounds of the Bondla Wildlife Sanctuary.*

grounds will also offer a glimpse of the resident troop of wild **macaque monkeys**, a rarity in the more heavily populated areas of Goa. The sanctuary also has a small restaurant and half a dozen tourist bungalows, making it a pleasant place to stay overnight on a longer exploration of Ponda province. A short stop at Bondla is included on a number of excursions operated by the Goa Tourist Development Corporation.

SANGUEM AND SURROUNDS

There isn't an awful lot to do in the little town of Sanguem so it would be wise to pass it by and head for Sanguem province's three main attractions.

Tambdi Surla Temple (Shri Mahadeva Temple) ★★★

This temple is 8km (5 miles) from **Molem** village and 3km (2 miles) from the smaller village of **Surla**. There is a real thrill of discovery in the approach to the temple which stands aloof from Goa's more populated areas on the verge of the thickly wooded **Western Ghats**, which form a dramatic backdrop. Set in a riverside clearing and surrounded by tropical forest, this is the only surviving

---

WILDLIFE

Hunting, poaching and deforestation together with ever-increasing population pressure have placed India's wildlife in great difficulty. Larger species such as tiger, elephant, leopard and rhinoceros are now confined to the country's network of wildlife reserves, of which there are now currently more than 100.

Above: *Goa's Hindu temples have often been restored and repaired, and work continues, so few of them show their true age.*

temple from the era of the Kadamba kings. Built between the 11th and 13th centuries, it looks far more satisfyingly ancient than the often modernized, European-influenced temples around Ponda.

The temple has two halls and an inner sanctuary, all standing on a raised plinth, with flights of steps leading to entrances on the north, south and east sides of the main hall. The plain exterior is decorated with stylized rosette reliefs. The *shikhara* (spire), now truncated, rises in three massive stone tiers above the sanctuary and displays remarkable carvings of Brahma, Shiva and Parvati. The temple is built of black basalt, which was preferred by Kadamba masons because it could be carved more cleanly and lasted far longer than the soft, crumbly laterite which is the only stone found in Goa. Importing the necessary stone, probably from Karnataka, must have been a considerable challenge. Ten plain pillars support the roof of the main hall, with four elaborately carved columns in the middle of the hall. The rear walls display niches for now-missing statues.

Rivona Caves *

About 5km (3 miles) from Sanguem town, a series of artificial caves carved in the rock were originally a **Buddhist monastery**. It was built around the 7th century AD and later taken over as Hindu shrines. These caves resemble mine shafts and one in particular is guarded by a worn 16th-century image of the ever-popular monkey-god **Hanuman**. The Hindu shrines don't really justify a special journey but are worth making the relatively short detour on the way to the more striking Tambdi Surla temple.

TEMPLE ETIQUETTE

All of Goa's Hindu temples are in use as places of worship. To avoid giving offence, visitors should dress modestly (skimpy beachwear is unacceptable). Footwear must be removed before entering the temple precincts so take a shoulder bag to deposit your shoes in. Many temples have a prominently placed collection box and a small donation will always be appreciated.

Baghwan Mahavir Wildlife Sanctuary ★★

This wildlife reserve is much larger than that at Bondla, covering 240km² (96 sq miles) of forested hills to the east of **Molem** village, in a prominent strip of territory jutting east towards the Karnataka border. It provides a refuge for Indian wildlife, including a large herd of **gaur**, **Indian elephant**, **leopard**, **black panther** and several species of **deer**. **Tigers** are reportedly sometimes seen by rangers, but are very rare and are always under threat from poachers.

Much of the reserve is covered by thick forest and the network of hiking trails and four-wheel-drive tracks is still incomplete. Eventually, it is planned to build a number of night hides with salt licks to attract larger, shyer animals. Most of the larger game animals keep to the trackless southern section, and at present are rarely spotted by visitors.

Below: *Leopard are protected in the forests of Baghwan Mahavir Wildlife Sanctuary, but are rarely seen.*

The park does, however, offer superb **birdwatching**, with virtually all the main South Indian species represented, and plenty of clear views over the lower, rolling grassland section of the park where gaur are sometimes seen as well as macaque and other common Indian monkeys.

The Goa Tourist Development Corporation operates a small number of rooms in tourist bungalows which are close to the main gate of the sanctuary, and an overnight stay allows you to join one of the morning and evening game drives. These drives offer the best chance of seeing game such as gaur, deer and, with luck, elephant.

Above: *The rail journey to Dudhsagar Falls offers fine views of the steep, wooded Western Ghats.*
Below: *The railway line to Karnataka passes Dudhsagar Falls, the highest in India.*

Dudhsagar Falls ★★★

The rail journey from Vasco da Gama or Margao to Dudhsagar Falls in Goa's western mountain ranges effectively gives the visitor a bargain-priced tour of the state. Departing from the station at Vasco not long after dawn, the train trundles through the countryside of coastal Marmagao and Salcete provinces to reach **Margao**, the largest town in southern Goa, about an hour later. Travellers from the south Goa coast resorts can join the train here. As the line winds eastward from Margao the countryside changes, and at **Kalem**, where the hills begin, a second engine is attached to push the train up the steepest stretch of track to the station at **Castle Rock**.

There are fine views back over the lowlands of Goa and along the vista of the Western Ghats as the train switchbacks through the hills, eventually arriving at Dudhsagar halt within sight of the falls high above and to the right of the track. The station shelter is at 241m (783ft) above sea level, but the falls start high above and plummet 600m (1950ft) to the foam-white pools below.

The falls are formed by the **Candepar River**, and are at their best in September, just after the end of the monsoon season, when they are at their fullest.

A path leads from the railway to the lower pool, where you can swim. The walk down is relatively easy but the 150m (500ft) zigzag ascent is taxing.

Unfortunately there are no refreshments at the falls or at the railway halt so bring a picnic and cold drinks from your hotel.

Eastern Goa at a Glance

As with other parts of Goa, the best time of the year to visit is from **mid-September** to **mid-February** when day-time temperatures average around 27°C (80°F).

To get to **Ponda** there are several daily **buses** from Panaji (1½ hours) and Margao (1 hour).
To **Sanguem** town you can take several daily buses from Margao (1½ hours). There are several **trains** daily from Vasco da Gama (3 hours) and Margao (2 hours) to **Dudhsagar Falls** which will take you directly to below the falls. You can also catch this train at Candolim or Dabolim, which may be more convenient if you are staying at one of the nearby south coast resorts. In order to get to the **Bagh-wan Mahavir Wildlife Sanctuary** catch the Dudhsagar train as far as Colem railway station, 3km (2 miles) from Molem village at the gateway to the park and then hire an **auto-rickshaw** or **motorbike** to the park entrance office.

The easiest way to explore Ponda and Sanguem is to rent a **car** with a driver from your resort or in Panaji, or to go on one of the organized tours (*see* Tours and Excursions). Public transport other than the **bus** and **train** is thin on the ground and you are unlikely to find even local yellow-topped **taxis**.

The only accommodation in the region is in the **Bondla** and **Baghwan Mahavir Wildlife Sanctuaries**, where the Goa Tourist Development Corporation maintains a small number of rather spartan but comfortable rooms in tourist bungalows. Availability is always limited, so if you plan to stay overnight it is essential that you book well in advance, preferably before leaving home. Reservations from:
Goa Tourist Development Corporation, Tourist Home, Pato, Panaji, tel: (022) 5583/5715/4757.

This is the least touristy part of Goa and there are no restaurants catering specifically for foreign visitors. Eating-places tend to be extremely simple and English is not widely spoken. If you are travelling on an organized tour a snack lunch and refreshments will probably be provided (though it is always best to check). If you are travelling by rail you can buy snacks and cold drinks from **vendors** at every station, or bring a pre-packed **picnic**. Most resort hotels and many restaurants are happy to provide this. The stainless-steel tiffin cans with wire handles sold in local stores and markets are an excellent way of carrying picnic meals. There are GTDC-run **restaurants** at both wildlife sanctuaries, but the menu is more limited than it would be in a restaurant at one of the beach resorts.

Daily tours of the temples are available from Panaji and main south coast resorts. Information and bookings from the GTDC or **Goa Tourist Development Corporation**, (see above).

There are no tourist or information offices outside Panaji; for information *see* p. 55, Central Goa and Panaji at a Glance.

EASTERN GOA	J	F	M	A	M	J	J	A	S	O	N	D
AVERAGE TEMP. °C	25	26	27	29	30	28	26	26	26	27	27	27
AVERAGE TEMP. °F	76	77	78	84	85	84	77	77	77	78	78	78
HOURS OF SUN DAILY	10	12	12	10	10	1	1	4	5	6	10	10
DAYS OF RAINFALL	1	0	1	8	9	30	30	30	20	10	5	5
RAINFALL mm	2	0	4	17	18	500	890	340	277	122	20	30
RAINFALL in	-	-	.15	.9	.9	20	36	14	11	5	.1	1.2

6
Southern Goa

Southern Goa has become increasingly popular since the flood of charter flights begun in the 1980s. Its beaches are the equal of any in the north, and despite the tourism boom are still generally less crowded. They also have the added advantage that, since there are no major rivers between the southern provinces and the airport at Dabolim, coach transfer times are much shorter.

Salcete province in the north borders Marmagao and is separated from Ponda by the upper Zuari River. **Quepem**, the next province south, is sandwiched between Salcete and Goa's southernmost province, **Canacona**. Salcete's coastline is a 20km (12½ miles) stretch of continuous sand which extends unbroken from **Cansaulim** to the mouth of the **Sal River** in the south. Cansaulim is administratively part of Marmagao province but as it is part of this southern beach strip it is included in this chapter.

Quepem, which has only a tiny section of seacoast between the mouth of the Sal River and the promontory of **Cabo de Rama** (Cape Rama), has all but escaped tourist attention and has no outstanding sightseeing attractions.

Canacona has until recently been the south's equivalent of Pernem province in the north: a last escape for those who are prepared to accept the simplest of food and accommodation in order to find the perfect beach and escape the tourism boom. Its relative inaccessibility has given it considerable immunity from development until now but with the construction of the coastal **Konkan** railway line its days of glorious isolation are numbered.

DON'T MISS

*** **Loutulim:** South Goa's prettiest traditional village.
*** **Colva:** the finest beach in Goa.
*** **Palolem:** last chance to see this unspoiled beach before development takes it over completely.
** **Chandrapura:** fascinating archaeological site.

Opposite: *Colva Beach offers spectacular sunsets over the Arabian Sea.*

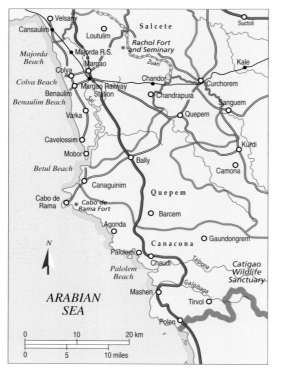

Margao (Madgaon) and Surrounds

Margao, the capital of **Salcete** province, is a sleepy market town and road-rail junction which only seems to wake up fully when its sprawling covered market is in full swing. Margao is first and foremost a farming town, and most foreigners pause here only to change buses on the way to or from the Salcete coast resorts, or perhaps to visit the market. Like Panaji, the town clearly displays its Portuguese heritage, especially in the town centre streets between **Jorge Barreto Park** and **Church Square**, which are lined by faded 18th- and 19th-century mansions.

Church of the Holy Spirit ★

The 17th-century Church of the Holy Spirit, built soon after the Portuguese conquest of Salcete, occupies one side of a square of once-grand colonial buildings. In the centre of the **Church Square** stands an ornate, white-washed monumental cross which is all that remains of the earlier, 16th-century church, destroyed in a Muslim attack only 14 years after its foundation in 1565. The present church dates from 1675 and has a florid, highly ornamented Baroque façade. To enter the church, walk through the archway on the south side. This leads to a courtyard which has been created by the surrounding clerical buildings. Notice the beautifully carved Indian Baroque altarpieces and the highly detailed sanctuary.

Rachol Fort and Seminary ★★

The seminary was transferred in 1580 from Margao, which had been repeatedly attacked by the Muslims, to the greater security of the fort at Rachol. Dating from the 14th-century, the fort was conquered by the **Raja of Vijayanagar** in 1520, and shortly afterwards ceded to his Portuguese allies, who turned it into their strongest inland fortification. By the mid-19th century, however, the threat of invasion by Muslim or Hindu neighbours was over, and the Portuguese decommissioned the fort and allowed its ramparts to crumble. There is now little left of the outer walls, which may have been quarried for stone to build the Rachol Seminary. This Catholic college became Goa's leading centre of learning and is still in service. Its dignified, dazzlingly white outer walls conceal a broad inner courtyard painted in a rather festive shade of pink. The enormous façade of the seminary church, which is similar within to Bom Jesus in Old Goa, occupies one entire side of the courtyard of the old college.

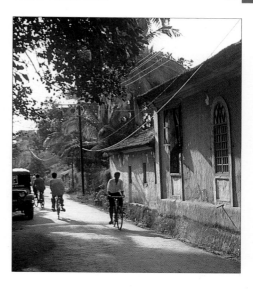

Above: *Stucco-fronted houses typical of the Portuguese colonial period line the sleepy streets of Margao.*

Loutulim ★★★

North of Margao is Loutulim, a strong contender for the title of prettiest village in Goa, with many delightfully attractive and well-preserved homes dating back to the heyday of the Portuguese empire. On a bright day, Loutulim can be blinding, with the sun blazing back from every whitewashed wall, highlighted by typically Goan touches of ochre and pink. The village radiates from a central square, overlooked by a delightful parish church, having a façade that is a fantasy of Baroque columns and arches.

MARATHA WARS

Portugal came closest to losing its Indian territories completely in their war with the Marathas of Maharashtra (1737–39). After capturing many of Portugal's northern strongholds, these fierce Hindu warriors swept into Goa itself, capturing Margao and threatening the capital. The Portuguese defence, however, was so stubborn that the Marathas agreed to a peace treaty in May 1739, though Portugal lost much of its territory in the north.

Above: *Goan villagers traditionally don brightly dyed new clothing for the many Hindu and Christian festivals which punctuate the year.*

Chandor *

The village of Chandor is 5km (3 miles) from Margao and is the site of one of Goa's colourful festivals, the **Fair of Reis Magos** (the Magi Kings or Three Wise Men), on 6 January each year. The village's central square is dominated by the vast arched frontage of one of the grand aristocratic homes which are characteristic of Salcete province. The **Menezes Braganza House** is open to the public and offers a fascinating glimpse of how wealthy Goan families lived in the 18th and 19th centuries, when the major part of this house was built. The Menezes Braganza family, early converts to the Roman Catholic faith, have lived here since the 16th century. The marble-floored grand salon, the large library, the banqueting hall, and private chapel are all indications of the family's considerable wealth and status.

Chandrapura *

The earliest ancient settlement to be discovered in Goa lies 2km (1¼ miles) from Chandor. The site of Chandrapura first drew the attention of archaeologists in 1929, and excavations since then indicate the **ancient fortress** and **temple** found here date back to the 3rd century BC. In the late 6th century this river port became the capital of the region under the **Kadamba** dynasty. In 1052 they moved their capital to Govalpuri between the Zuari and Mandovi rivers – the exact site is not known. Considerable imagination is needed to picture the substantial city which once stood here, as all that remains are the stone foundations of the fortress and the brick walls of a temple to **Shiva** which stood within.

DHOBI

The Indian *dhobi* (laundry) system never fails to astonish first-time visitors. In a country where many services – such as hotel and airline reservations, telephones and every aspect of government bureaucracy – work slowly and unreliably if at all, the *dhobi walla* (laundry man) is a shining example of superbly efficient service at a very low price. Nowhere else in the world can you get your clothes washed so quickly, cheaply and efficiently – and all by hand.

SOUTHERN BEACH VILLAGES

Goa's longest beach – and one of the finest in Asia – starts just south of the **Bogmalo** headland in Marmagao province and seems to go on almost forever. Hotels and small resorts are scattered along its 25km (15 mile) length, clustering around former fishing villages. Most of them are set several hundred metres back from the beach for protection from the powerful waves which lash and clean the beach during the summer monsoon. A coastal highway runs parallel to the shore as far as the **Sal** estuary, connecting this string of villages. From mid-1996 the new **Konkan** railway line is scheduled to run through southern Salcete province to Margao, connecting this part of Goa with points south. Predictably, tourism development is gradually filling the gaps between villages but there are still long stretches of near-deserted sand between the little clusters of restaurants and guesthouses.

Left: *Tourist money attracts troops of young beach vendors to drive a hard bargain on Benaulim beach.*

CASHEWS

Brought to India by the Portuguese, the cashew trees which cover much of inland Goa are one of Goa's biggest export earners. Roasted cashews which are sold loose in bulk in most markets are a good buy to take home. Cashews are also made into *feni*, which is distilled from juice pressed from the bright yellow fruit.

Above: *Slender palm trees line the high water mark along the majestic sweep of Colva beach.*

Cansaulim ★★

Not to be confused with Candolim, in Bardez province, this village marks the northern beginning of south Goa's fabulous beach strip. From here the beach blends seamlessly with Colva, and the sands then run unbroken as far as the Sal River. Because of its proximity to **Dabolim Airport**, which is accessible by road and rail, Cansaulim is amongst the busiest of the small southern Goan resorts, but still far quieter than the more popular resorts of northern Goa.

Majorda ★★

Majorda is situated 5km (3 miles) south of Cansaulim and set some 2km (1¼ miles) inland from the beach. Majorda also has a railway station, making it easily accessible. Like Cansaulim, its beach is its main attraction, but a late 18th-century **Church of Our Lady** lends the village some historic interest.

Colva ★★★

Colva village, midway along the stretch of beach which bears its name, is about 8km (5 miles) west of **Margao**, the provincial capital. Set about 1.5km (1 mile) inland from the beach, it has grown into the biggest village on the southern coast and is the hub of a string of hotels and

restaurants, spreading along the beach to north and
south. Though the village has already come a long way
since the 1960s, when it was little more than a fishing
settlement and favoured by low-budget independent
travellers, it is still far from being overdeveloped by
international resort standards. Most of the hotels are
fairly small, and much of the accommodation available
still caters for the less well-heeled traveller as well as to
mid-market package holidaymakers. In fact, most of the
development is driven by the Indian domestic tourism
market and Colva is far from being overwhelmed by the
international package holiday business. Canoe-like fishing boats no longer line the beach, as most of the local
fishermen have invested in sturdier wooden tubs that
bob at anchor just offshore. A church of **Our Lady of
Mercy** stands at the village crossroads. Typically brilliant
white on the exterior, it has a gaudy ornately decorated
interior. Founded in 1630, the church was rebuilt by the
Jesuit order during the 18th century.

Benaulim ★★★

Benaulim village, immedi-
ately south of Colva, is
landmarked by the hilltop
church of **St John the
Baptist**, which stands
above the village about
1km (⅔ mile) inland from
the beach. This is the
quietest section of the
southern coast, with few
hotels of any size, and
remains a favourite with
independent travellers.
Further south, small
guesthouses and beach
restaurants are dotted
along the sections of beach
close to the inland villages
of **Varca** and **Cavelossim**.

> **KITES**
>
> The buzzard-like, carrion-
> eating kites are frequently
> seen circling above villages
> and fields. Commonest
> around towns and villages
> is the **pariah kite** with dark
> brown plumage and a promi-
> nent forked tail. Along the
> coast and around lakes and
> rivers look out for the slightly
> smaller **Brahminy kite**, with
> a rounded tail, chestnut
> wings and black and
> white head and breast.

Below: *Water buffalo are
used to plough Goa's green
and gold rice fields.*

Mobor **

Mobor village stands on the narrow northern headland at the mouth of the **Sal River**, marking the southern end of the Salcete province beach strip. Despite its relative remoteness, this is the most upmarket resort in southern Goa, with a clutch of expensive, top-notch hotels set in immaculately manicured grounds. Unless you are staying in one of these resort complexes, however, Mobor does not offer much to see or do. There are virtually no facilities for visitors in Mobor village and it remains little more than a ramshackle fishing hamlet. Keen birders, though, will find the Sal River estuary attracts many species of seabirds and waterfowl, including huge flocks of gulls and several species of kingfisher, stork and heron.

Betul **

Quepem province is almost landlocked, with only a short stretch of coast between the Sal estuary and the provincial border with Canacona province to the south. Betul is the province's only beach settlement. Getting to this settlement, on the south shore of the Sal estuary,

Below: *Peddlars on the beach at Benaulim.*

entails a detour inland to the foot-bridge or ferry crossing. The visitor in search of the impossible dream of an as-yet-untouched Goan beach will find the journey well worthwhile. The minor inconvenience of crossing the river has saved Betul from tourism, at least for the time being, and it is very much a village for travellers seeking a perfect beach and the simplest of food and accommodation. Unlike most of the Goan fishing settlements, Betul is built close to the high-tide line as the Sal headland protects it from the worst of the monsoon gales. It is also within easy reach of the equally fine, peaceful beaches of Canacona province next door, from which it is separated by the rocky headland of **Cabo de Rama**.

Above: *Beach umbrellas at peaceful Mobor are a sign of increasing tourism encroachment.*

CANACONA

Goa's most southerly province, bordered by Karnataka state to the south, is its quietest and least developed. Until recently, its superb, untouched beaches and tiny fishing villages attracted only the most determined of travellers: those who were prepared to accept a very basic standard of living, use uncomfortable local public transport, and dispense with all the tourist trimmings. The opening of the **Konkan** railway, connecting the province with Margao and the 20th century, is set to change everything, though perhaps not overnight.

In the meantime, Canacona's **beaches** – a series of crescent-shaped sweeps of sand separated by headlands and backed by hills – remain idyllic. Its hilly hinterland, much of which is given over to the **Catigao Wildlife Sanctuary**, is one of Goa's great escapes and is drama-

EGRETS

These white-plumed relatives of the heron are seen everywhere in paddy fields and among cattle. Commonest is the **cattle egret**, tall and recognizable by its orange upper plumage in the breeding season and by its yellow beak and legs. It feeds in cattle fields, often perching on the animals' backs, and in village trash heaps. Similar but slightly larger is the **little egret**, which has black beak and legs and stalks its prey in shallow water. Also seen in ponds, lakes and flooded fields is the **large egret**, with a yellow beak and black legs.

Above: *Palm trees fringe a magnificent sunset at Palolem, one of Goa's remotest beach villages.*

ROLLERS AND BEE-EATERS

Among the most colourful birds of the Indian country-side, the roller has a turquoise-green back and wings, a deep blue tail and a pinkish breast, with purple touches on the neck and nape. It is seen either perching on wires or branches in open country, or in distinctive gliding, swooping flight. The related green bee-eater is even more vivid, with bright green plumage, blue chin and throat, and a yellowish head.

---

tically different from the pastoral scenes of the central provinces. It was among the last segments of present-day Goa to be added to the Portuguese colony, being taken over by treaty from the **King of Sunda** in 1791.

Chaudi is Canacona province's administrative centre and transport hub, but has no facilities for visitors and no sights to visit. It's really no more than a place to change buses. From late 1996, however, it is scheduled to become the province's main station on the Konkan railway line, and this will no doubt bring about many changes to villages along the new track.

Cabo de Rama ★

Cabo de Rama (Cape Rama) juts into the Arabian Sea close to Canacona's border with Quepem province. Its strategic advantages were obvious from the earliest times, and according to local legend the warrior-god **Rama** took refuge here after being defeated by his demonic enemies. In historic times, the site attracted the attention first of the local rulers, then of the Portuguese, who seized the fort from the **King of Sunda** in 1763 and added a small chapel – which can still be seen inside the ramparts – and substantial barrack buildings, which have crumbled into a maze of roofless walls. A deep ditch was the first line of defence, and is overlooked by massive, crumbling walls and the tumbledown remains of the main gate. The stronghold has been disused since the 1830s, when the Portuguese abandoned it.

Palolem **

Some people think Palolem is the best beach in Goa. It is certainly one of the most visually appealing. A 1.5km (1 mile) curve of glowing gold sand is hemmed in by thickly wooded headlands. Offshore is a tiny islet which you can walk to at low tide. Coconut palms and a clutter of tiny, brightly painted beach bars line the top of the beach. Palolem village is little more than a line of shops, homes, and very simple restaurants either side of the road which connects the coast with Chaudi, the provincial capital.

Below: *The long-tailed Macaque may be found in the Catigao Wildlife sanctuary.*

Catigao Wildlife Sanctuary *

Catigao Wildlife Sanctuary is a 100km² (40 sq mile) slice of hilly, forested land in the low foothills of the **Western Ghats**. It is undoubtedly the wildest of Goa's three sanctuaries, but is not very user-friendly. In order to explore it properly you must bring your own vehicle (preferably four-wheel drive as there is only one dirt track within the sanctuary) or explore the area on foot. There are no food or lodging facilities.

Southern Goa at a Glance

BEST TIMES TO VISIT

As with other parts of Goa, **mid-September** to **mid-February** is the most favourable time to visit because the daytime temperatures average around 27°C (80°F).

GETTING THERE

There are several daily **buses** to Margao from Panaji (2 hours) and Vasco da Gama (1 hour and 30 mins). Several daily **trains** (1 hour and 30 mins) arrive in Margao from Vasco da Gama.

Trains travelling between Vasco da Gama and Margao also stop at Cansaulim and Majorda stations (about 25 minutes and 35 minutes respectively) for the southern beach villages.

The new **Konkan railway**, currently under construction, is scheduled to connect Margao with Chaudi and points south, making onward travel to Karnataka State and Kerala much easier and more efficient.

Buses from Vasco to Cansaulim take around 45 minutes and buses to Majorda take approximately 55 minutes. There are several buses daily from Margao to Colva and Benaulim (15 minutes) and to Mobor (30 minutes). For Betul, take the Mobor bus and cross the Sal River by the ferry or footbridge at the end of the paved road.

There are several buses daily from Margao (1 hour) to Chaudi in Canacona as well as the rail service to Margao on the Konkan line. Getting to the fort at Cabo de Rama and the tiny neighbouring village involves either renting your own transport or a long walk from the nearest main road between Betul and Chaudi. Two buses daily leave from Chaudi for Palolem (30 minutes).

GETTING AROUND

Bicycles, small **motorcycles** and **taxis** can be hired from the larger Colva beach resorts. One of the best ways to explore the full length of the south coast beach strip is by motorcycle. Elsewhere, public transport is limited to **buses**.

WHERE TO STAY

Salcete
LUXURY
Majorda Beach Resort, Majorda, tel: 20025, 20751, 20321, 21181 (there are no codes available for any hotels. Please ask the operator to help you). This is a luxury 63-room resort with 10 self-contained villas.

Ramada Renaissance Resort, Colva Beach, tel: 23611/12. International chain resort with 130 rooms, nine-hole golf course and tennis courts. Self sufficient

and extremely well managed, if rather sterile.

Leela Beach Goa, Mobor, Cavelossim, tel: 08344 6363, fax: 08344 6352. A member of the prestigious **Leading Hotels of the World** consortium, the Leela Beach is southern Goa's most luxurious resort, set in 18.2ha (45 acres) of beautiful landscaped gardens.

MID-RANGE
Holiday Inn Resort, Mobor Beach, Cavelossim, tel: 91834 246303/06, fax: 91834 246333. Friendly atmosphere. Comfortable resort with 150 rooms.

Goa Penta, Utorda, Majorda Beach, tel: 23978. A delightfully pleasant hotel which is managed by an international chain. It consists of 105 rooms.

Dona Sylvia, Cavelossim Beach, tel: 0834 246321/28, fax: 0834 246320. Low-rise village-style resort with 174 rooms in 68 Mediterranean-style bungalows, set in beautiful landscaped grounds.

The Old Anchor, Cavelossim Beach, tel: 0834 246337/44. Large medium-priced hotel of 240 rooms close to the southern end of the Colva beach strip.

Southern Goa at a Glance

BUDGET

Colva Tourist Cottages, Colva village, tel: 08342 222287 and 362144. Two separate government-run units of 18 rooms and 49 rooms respectively. Accommodation is simple and very cheap, with a choice of single, two- and three-bed rooms and dormitories.

Betul

As yet Betul has only the most simple accommodation and finding a place to stay is just a matter of turning up and asking around.

Canacona

Palolem is poised on the brink of development, with sites being pegged out for several small hotels. At present, however, accommodation consists of some rooms in private homes and a very basic campsite hidden among trees near the beach.

WHERE TO EAT

Salcete Beach villages

There are far too many beach shacks, bars and café-restaurants along this whole stretch of beach to list them all individually, and as the scene is constantly changing – with new places springing up and old places changing hands or changing their names –

any attempt to do so or to single out individual places can only be misleading. Most have a very similar bill of fare, on which seafood figures prominently. Most places to eat and drink are on or close to the beach, not in the villages which are set inland from the beach. Be warned that during the early June to early September monsoon season almost all of these close down as well as many hotels and guesthouses which depend on the package holiday trade. The main concentrations of places to eat outside the large resort hotels are at Cansaulim, Majorda, Colva, and Benaulim.

Betul

There are only a handful of very simple restaurants on the beach and along the village main street. The best option would be to try them yourself.

Canacona

Chaudi: There are a few snack and cold drinks stalls close to the bus stop on Chaudi's main street.

Palolem

Several simple beach restaurants and bars are scattered along Palolem's crescent-shaped beach.

TOURS AND EXCURSIONS

Tours and excursions to attractions in southern and central Goa are offered by most of the larger hotels in Colva and other beach resorts. The favourite destinations amongst visitors include half-day tours of **Old Goa** and its many beautiful, historic cathedrals, the colourful Hindu temples of the **Ponda** region, and the full-day rail trip to the incredibly spectacular **Dudhsagar Falls**.

USEFUL CONTACTS

Government of Goa Tourist Information Office, Tourist Home, Patto, Panaji, tel: (022) 45583, 45715, 44757. Services include: leaflets, maps, list of hotels and guesthouses, bookings for state-run hotels and wildlife reserve bungalows, excursions and ferry bookings.

SOUTHERN GOA	J	F	M	A	M	J	J	A	S	O	N	D
AVERAGE TEMP. °C	25	26	27	29	30	28	26	26	26	27	27	27
AVERAGE TEMP. °F	76	77	78	84	85	84	77	77	77	78	78	78
HOURS OF SUN DAILY	10	12	12	10	10	1	1	4	5	6	10	10
DAYS OF RAINFALL	1	0	1	8	9	30	30	30	20	10	5	5
RAINFALL mm	2	0	4	17	18	500	890	340	277	122	20	30
RAINFALL in	-	-	.15	.9	.9	20	36	14	11	5	.1	1.2

7
Karnataka and Kerala

It has been claimed that Goa, with its Portuguese colonial heritage, is the least Indian of India's many states. If this is the case, the regions around it will perhaps bear a closer resemblance to the India many visitors imagine: **Karnataka**, with its splendid palaces from the great days of the Muslim princes and magnificent temples; **Kerala**, with its fine beaches and vast stretches of inland waterways; and the vast state of **Maharashtra**, heartland of the great Maratha empire. Each of these destinations offers a taste of a very different India; each has its own language, customs and costume, and a journey onward from Goa can be far more satisfying than a simple beach-based holiday.

Until recently, adding a trip to one of these neighbouring destinations onto a holiday in Goa posed a few problems. Overland travel is time-consuming. The rail journey from Goa to **Bangalore** in eastern Karnataka, for example, takes almost 24 hours and until recently air travel was unreliable as flights were very often overbooked or cancelled. In recent years there has however been a vast improvement in regional air services, and flights from Goa to destinations in Karnataka and Kerala are now much more reliable and competitively priced. In addition, Kerala has become a holiday haven in its own right (and a competitor to Goa) with direct charter flights from European cities arriving in the favoured southern resort of **Trivandrum** in the winter, which has the feel of an overgrown village despite its size.

· Don't Miss

*** Hambi: ruined 14th century city with many Hindu temples and palaces.
*** Bijapur: former capital of the great 15th century Muslim empire of Bijapur.
*** Aihole, Pattadakal and **Badami:** treasuries of Hindu temple architecture dating from the 5th, 6th and 7th centuries.
** Bangalore: Karnataka's cosmopolitan big city.
** Mysore: historic city with a rich royal heritage.

Opposite: *The magnificent palace of the Maharajahs of Mysore.*

KARNATAKA

Karnataka, which borders Goa to the south and east, is a vast state which covers just over 190,000km² (73,340 sq miles) and is home to almost 45 million people. The most widely spoken language is **Kannada**. Much of the state is rolling plateau country, cut off from the coast by the steep ranges of the **Western Ghats**. The state has its own little-developed beaches but these are not very easy to get to and offer none of the facilities of the Goan and Keralan coasts. For the visitor travelling onward from Goa, Karnataka's main attractions are the historic cities and ruined temples and fortresses scattered throughout the region.

Among the most interesting sights in northern Karnataka are the relics of the **kingdoms of Muslim Bijapur** and **Hindu Vijayanagar**, whose rulers vied for control of Goa over several centuries. **Mysore**, in the southern part of the state, is also well worth a visit.

Above: *Though Karnataka is one of India's richest states, age-old transport methods are still used.*

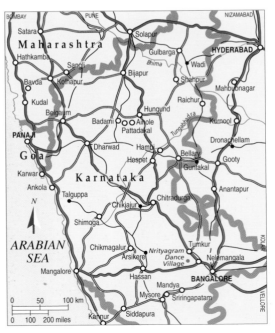

The contrasts between traditional and modern India are perhaps stronger here than anywhere else in the south. In rural villages the ox-drawn plough and cart are still the norm and farming is still labour intensive. However, **Bangalore**, the state capital, is the proud centre of India's space programme and a computer industry which exports millions of dollars worth of sophisticated software via satellite to customers in Asia, Europe and the United States of America, earning the region the nickname 'Silicon Plateau'.

Karnataka is also quite a way off the most heavily travelled tourist routes, and visitors arriving from the more frequently visited cities of northern India will find very little of the high-pressure touting which surrounds the country's more popular sightseeing destinations.

Hampi **

The ruined capital of the mighty 14th century **Vijayanagar** empire is 13km (6 miles) from the modern town of **Hospet** and 330km (205 miles) northeast of Bangalore. Now a UNESCO World Heritage Centre, it is the most striking of the region's ruined cities, landmarked by towering temple *ziggurats* (towers). Restoration of its superb collection of temples and palaces continues. Set against a backdrop of rugged, rocky hills, the city is surrounded on three sides by the **Tungabhadra River**. Remnants of its seven rings of ramparts can still be seen. Within them, the kings of Vijayanagar ruled their empire from a city of half a million people, defended by a mighty army. Founded in 1336, the empire reached its zenith in the early 16th century, when it controlled virtually all of southern India. The end came in 1565, when it was sacked by a Muslim army.

Below: *A bearded sadhu (Hindu holy man) sounds a traditional conch shell trumpet to announce a Hindu feast day.*

Hampi's Sights

The oversized set of scales which stood at the **King's Balance** were used annually to weigh the king against the tribute of gold and precious stones brought to him, which was then donated to the city temples. Remnants of frescoes and carved friezes decorate the square stone tank known as the **Queen's Bath** which was once covered by a vaulted canopy. The **Lotus Mahal** is a two-storey building next to the Queen's Bath and is a pretty mixture of Muslim and Hindu influences. It housed the royal ladies-in-waiting.

Built on an appropriately vast scale, the 10 vaulted chambers of the **Elephant Stables** surround a central pavilion which housed the keepers of the royal elephants. The most glorious of the city's temples, the **Vithala Temple** is noted for its series of columns, each carved from a single piece of rock and each chiming a different note when struck. Other highlights include a stone temple chariot drawn by elephants. Still used by Hindu worshippers, the temple to **Virupaksha** (one of the aspects of Shiva) is the most prominent building on the site. Its two courtyards are dominated by a huge stone **gopuram** (gateway) some 50m (164 ft) in height. The 6.7m (22ft) monolith of **Ugra Narasimha** depicts Vishnu in his incarnation as Narasimha, the mythical half-lion, half-man.

Below: *The massive temple chariot carved from stone is a highlight of Vithala.*

Bijapur ★

Bijapur, in northern Karnataka, 530km (331 miles) north of Bangalore and 200km (125 miles) from Hampi, was the inland capital of the **Adil Shahi** dynasty who wrested Goa and much of the region from the control of **Vijayanagar** during the 15th century. Its treasury of graceful Islamic architecture, dating from the 16th and 17th centuries, is strikingly different from the massive temples of contemporary Hindu sites, and is equally impressive.

Bijapur's Sights

One of the world's largest unsupported domes, the Gol Gumbaz houses the tomb of **Mohammed Adil Shah III** (1626–56). Its remarkable acoustics carry the slightest sound across the vast interior space. **Jumma Masjid**, a glorious mosque, with its gleaming gold dome and slender minarets, is one of the finest in India. Built by the first Adil Shah (1557–80), its proudest possession is a gold-lettered copy of the Koran and gilt Koranic verses which decorate the interior.

Claimed to have inspired the Taj Mahal, the **Ibrahim Roza** was built by Ibrahim Adil Shah II (1580–1626) as a mausoleum for his wife, the Taj Sultana. **Malik-e-Maidan**, a vast bronze artillery piece, 4m (14ft) long and weighing more than 50 tons, was seized as a war trophy from the rival kings of Purandar. The name means 'ruler of the plains'.

Above: *The Ibrahim Roza, built as a sultana's tomb, is claimed to have inspired the more famous Taj Mahal.*

Aihole, Pattadakal and Badami

These three superb temple towns – successively capitals of the Hindu Chalukya kings in the 5th, 6th and 7th centuries – lie within a 13km (8 mile) radius of one another. Located 125km (78 miles) north of Hampi and 75km (48 miles) south of Bijapur, they can be visited en route between the two.

Aihole, known as the 'cradle of Indian temple architecture', has 125 intricately carved Hindu temples. The oldest, the Lad Khan Temple, dates from the 5th century AD. **Pattadakal**, now a World Heritage Centre, has 10 fine temples, of which the most impressive is the vast **Virupaksha Temple**, dating from the 8th century. **Badami** is best known for four splendid cave temples with walls adorned by huge carvings of Shiva, Vishnu and other gods.

Below: *The massive Vidhana Soudha, home to Bangalore's Secretariat and State Legislature.*
Opposite: *Elaborate arches and colonnades grace the interior of the small elegant Palace of Tipu Sultan in Bangalore.*

BANGALORE

Founded by the Hindu ruler **Kempegowda** in 1537 and strengthened by the Muslim sultan **Hyder Ali** and his heir **Tipu Sultan**, Bangalore is one of India's most modern cities. At 1000m (3250ft) above sea level, its clement climate made it a favourite with the British after their conquest of the region from Tipu in 1799. By urban Indian standards, it is strikingly green with several fine public parks and gardens and a cosmopolitan laid-back air which sets it apart from other south Indian cities.

Sultan's Palace ★★

Originally within the walls of the sultan's fort, the small two-storey palace with its arches and arcades was begun by **Hyder Ali** in 1778. His heir finished the work the following year. Open 06:00–18:00 daily except on public holidays.

The Fort ★★

Massive stone bastions and ramparts mark the site of the stronghold, first of the 16th century king **Kempegowda** and later of the 18th century **Muslim** sultans. There is little to see within the walls. Open 08:00 to sunset, daily.

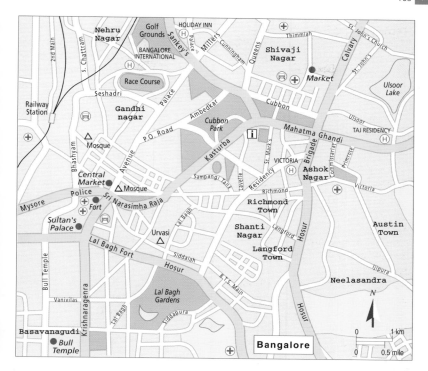

Bull Temple **

Within Bangalore's oldest temple stands the massive 4.6m (15ft) statue of the sacred bull **Nandi**, carved from a single block of granite polished to a gleaming black. The temple dates from **Kempegowda**'s 16th-century reign.

Lal Bagh Gardens *

The 100ha (240 acre) gardens were laid out by **Hyder Ali** in 1760 and further enlarged by his son **Tipu Sultan**. They are among the finest public gardens in India but are perhaps less impressive to the foreigner.

Cubbon Park *

The 121ha (300 acre) city-centre gardens were laid out in 1864 and named after the British Commissioner of Mysore state, Lieutenant General Sir Mark Cubbon (1784–1861).

Nrityagram Dance Village ★★

Some 30km (20 miles) outside Bangalore is this unique village where young women from all over India come to learn ancient dance forms through *guru-shishya parampara*, the age-old system whereby the tradition, culture and values of centuries are transmitted by word of mouth from teacher (*guru*) to disciple (*shishya*). You can watch dancers at their lessons and take part in yoga and meditation classes.

TIPU SULTAN

Tipu Sultan of Mysore was the last of the Indian rulers to resist the British. He was an astute politician as well as a competent general. Hiring European mercenaries to train his Muslim troops, he also allied himself with the French against the British in India. In 1799, commanded by **Lord Wellesley** (later the Duke of Wellington), the British invaded in force, and Tipu was killed in the battle for his fortress at **Seringapatam**.

MYSORE

Mysore, 140km (90 miles) southwest of Bangalore, is one of southern India's most appealing cities. Like Bangalore, its climate is comparatively temperate, thanks to its location 770m (2526ft) above sea level. The Wodeyar maharajahs became rulers of the city and the surrounding region during the 14th century. They were driven out by **Hyder Ali** in 1759 but regained the city 40 years later after the overthrow of **Tipu Sultan** and his French allies by the British in 1799. The **Wodeyars** then became rulers of the entire state under British tutelage and remained so until Independence. The city owes most of its striking landmarks to its princely rulers.

Royal Palace ★★★

When the maharajah's palace was gutted by fire in 1897, he commissioned the British architect **Henry Irwin** to build a new one. The work was completed in 1912. The palace is a glorious mixture of styles. Within, it seems to owe as much to Arabian Nights-style fantasy as to the formal Indo-Saracenic school of architecture. There are mosaic floors, silver doors, a solid gold throne weighing 200kg (440lb), and jewel-studded furniture. Gilt and crystal clash with gaudily painted walls and columns. Visit the palace again at nightfall, when the fabulous façade is illuminated by thousands of electric bulbs against a velvety black sky! Open 10:30–17:30, daily.

Below: *The dazzling display at the Royal Palace.*
Opposite: *Brightly coloured dye catches the eye in Bangalore's sprawling Central Market.*

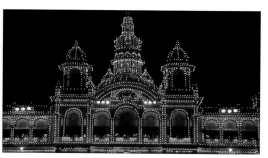

Sri Jayachamarajendra Art Gallery
(Jaganmohan Palace) *

The palace, built in 1861, was transformed into an art gallery in 1875. Exhibits include paintings by Indian and foreign artists, portraits of the royal family, and, most interestingly, traditional Mysore works in gold leaf. Open 08:00–17:30 daily.

Railway Museum *

Close to Mysore's splendid railway station (built for the maharajahs) is the **Mysore Railway Museum**, with a collection of locomotives and rolling stock which includes 19th-century carriages from the royal train of the Maharajah of Mysore, as well as an exhibition of historic railway paraphernalia. Open 08:00–17:00 daily.

Chamundi Hill
(Sri Chamundeswari
Temple) *

A thousand steps lead from the foot of this hill, 13km (8 miles) from the city, to the 2000-year-old temple dedicated to the Wodeyar dynasty's patron goddess, **Chamundeswari**. Halfway to the top stands a massive 4.8m (15ft) stone Nandi bull. You can cheat by taking a bus or taxi to the top of the hill.

Sriringapatam
(Seringapatam) *

Situated 16km (10 miles) north of Mysore, this town was the 18th-century capital of the great Muslim leader

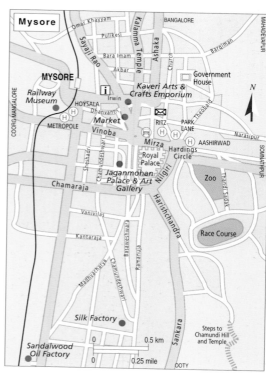

SANDALWOOD

Mysore is India's incense capital, with the scent of dozens of small incense factories perfuming many city streets. You can visit one of the city's many incense workshops to watch the fragrant sticks and cones being made by hand at terrific speed (enquire at KSTDC information office for details).

Above: *Fishermen enliven the beach scene for tourists at Kovalim.*

Below: *Palm trees line the Kerala backwaters.*

Hyder Ali Sultan and his son Tipu Sultan, who was killed in battle with the British here in 1799. They endowed the city with a treasury of striking buildings, including Tipu's splendid tomb, the **Gumbaz**, and his lovely summer palace, the **Dariya Daulat** – now a museum with an exhibition of the Sultan's possessions, portraits and weapons. Also worth seeing are the mighty ramparts of Tipu's fort. Set on an island in the **Cauvery River**, the town was founded by Hindu builders in the 13th century and among its architectural gems is the temple of **Ranganath**.

KERALA

Kerala is one of India's smaller states, with a population of around 30 million and a land area of roughly 40,000km² (15,500 sq miles). The most widely spoken local language is **Malayalam**. The state shares some of Goa's physical characteristics, forming a ribbon of verdant coastland where coconut palms, rice and cashew nuts are the main crops and many people make their living from fishing. Despite early contacts with the Europeans, however, Kerala did not share Goa's colonial history. It was created within its present borders after independence by merging part of the former province of **Madras** with two princely states, **Cochin** (now Kochi) and **Travancore**, which had been under British sway since the late 18th century. Kerala is also one of India's best-run states, with almost 60% literacy and the country's lowest infant mortality rate – significant achievements of an enlightened Marxist state government which has been in power on and off for some 40 years. Additional prosperity comes from the United Arab Emirates and other Gulf states, where many local men go to work for high wages (by Indian standards). Bright new cottages built with the earnings of these overseas workers line the coastal highway.

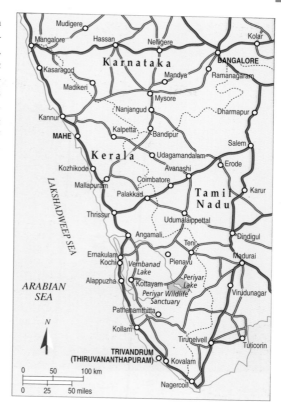

Because of its superb natural harbour at **Kochi** (Cochin), Kerala has long been exposed to the influence of the world beyond India. It was visited by ancient Greeks and Romans, Jews and Arabs before the arrival of the first Portuguese and Dutch fleets in the 16th century. Vasco da Gama's first expedition to India in search of 'spices and Christians' found a long-established Christian community, reputedly converted by St Thomas in the 1st century AD.

DON'T MISS

*** **Kovalam:** the finest beach in Kerala and one of the best in India.
*** **Kochi:** historic city on a spectacular natural harbour.
*** **Kerala backwaters:** delightful boat journey through palm-fringed tropical lagoons.

Fine beaches line Kerala's coast, stretching almost as far as India's southern tip. The state also has a growing tourism industry, with winter-season charter flights from several European airports to **Trivandrum** (Thiruvananthapuram) as well as a growing holiday resort area around **Kovalam**.

Trivandrum and Surrounds ★★

The capital of Kerala state is a pleasant, relaxed city in its own way, with distinctive local architecture and none of the urban pressure associated with most bigger Indian cities. That said, it has no major sightseeing attractions. The pleasant little **Napier Museum**, close to the city centre, is worth a visit. It has a small collection of bronze statues, carvings and ornate Hindu temple decorations.

For most visitors, the main attraction is the superb beach at **Kovalam**, some 16km (10 miles) south and rapidly becoming a favourite with European package holidaymakers in search of winter sunshine. Like Goa's beaches, Kovalam was an early favourite with low-budget backpackers but the influx of more upmarket tourists has changed its character. There are many new hotels, restaurants and souvenir shops springing up. Kovalam's beaches consist of a chain of three bays separated by a series of headlands.

KERALA FACTS AND FIGURES

With a population of over 30 million and a land area of 38,900km² (15,015 sq miles), Kerala is one of India's smaller states. Malayalam is the main language, and one in four Keralites is Christian.

Fishing, and coir fibre manufacture are important local industries and tourism is rapidly becoming a major foreign currency earner.

KOCHI (COCHIN) AND SURROUNDS

A deep natural harbour protected by an array of islands and peninsulas made Kochi one of India's most important cities in ancient times. It was one of the first points of contact between Portugal and India in the early 16th century. A century later, the Dutch ousted the Portuguese, only to be driven out in turn by the British at the beginning of the 18th century during the French Revolutionary Wars.

Each of these colonial powers ruled in alliance with the rajas of the **Varma** dynasty, who remained nominal rulers of Kochi until Independence. Today it remains an economically and strategically vital anchorage for merchant shipping and the Indian navy. The oldest part of the city, **Fort Kochi**, is on the main peninsula south of the harbour mouth. Between it and the more modern city, Ernakulam, on the mainland side of the harbour, is the artificial **Willingdon Island**, created from sand dredged out to improve navigation. **Vypeen Island** and **Bolgatty Island**, in the northern half of the bay, are connected to Fort Kochi, Ernakulam and each other by a fleet of ferry-boats and water-taxis.

The trip across the harbour is well worth taking, with fine views of the old and new parts of the port, where container vessels and Indian Navy frigates share the waves with tiny fishing canoes and rice barges. The city's main sightseeing attractions are in **Fort Kochi**, which with its narrow streets, whitewashed buildings and old warehouses and shops, is a great place to wander about. The most attractive part of the old town is **Jewtown**, the area around the historic synagogue.

> **CHRISTIANS IN KERALA**
>
> Kerala's Christians claim to be the first converts in India, having heard the word from **St Thomas**, who is said to have landed in Kerala in 52AD, travelling across southern India to Madras, where he was martyred in 68AD and is reputed to be buried.
>
> These earliest Christians were reinforced in later centuries by Christian traders and missionaries from the Middle East, but were then cut off from the rest of Christendom by the Muslim conquests in India.

Opposite: *Kovalam beach in Kerala is as popular with local people and fishermen as with the tourists who are now discovering it.*

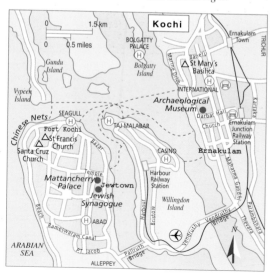

Chinese Nets ★★★

These wonderful contraptions which line the foreshore at the Fort Kochi side of the harbour mouth were introduced to the region by 14th-century Chinese traders. A gigantic dip-net is suspended from a complex wooden framework some 10m (30ft) high. The weight of the net is balanced out by heavy boulders. Each net is worked by a crew of three or four, and the catch is surprisingly small – a couple of dozen silvery pomfret for each dip of the net. It seems a lot of work for little gain.

Above: *Silhouetted against a sunset, Kochi's Chinese fishing nets are said to have been introduced by Chinese traders seven centuries ago.*
Below: *The small Mattancherry Palace in Kochi contains fine mural paintings of scenes from the Hindu epics.*

Mattancherry Palace (Dutch Palace) ★★★

The original two-storey palace was built by the Portuguese in 1557 in a bid to curry favour with the Raja of Cochin, **Veera Varma** (1537–61). The Dutch, also keen to gain the good graces of the Rajas, rebuilt it in the second half of the 17th century. The portraits of the Varma Rajas in the upper gallery show a strong family resemblance, from Rama Varma II (1864–88) to his last inheritor, Rama Varma VII (1948–64). The Rajas gave audience seated on a huge platform-swing which is

displayed on the first floor along with portraits and ceremonial dress. Some fine murals, depicting scenes from the *Ramayana* and other great Hindu epics, decorate many of the rooms. Leave enough time to examine them in some detail, as each vivid, action-packed section tells a story. Open 08:00–17:00 daily.

Jewish Synagogue ★★

This remarkable building was erected in 1664 on the site of an earlier synagogue by Kochi's long-established Jewish community, the descendants of traders from Palestine who first established links with India almost 2000 years ago. Polished brass pillars support the roof, from which dangle dozens of crystal chandeliers. Open 08:00–17:00 Monday–Thursday.

St Francis Church *

India's oldest church dates from 1403, when it was built by **Franciscans** who arrived with one of the earliest Portuguese expeditions. There is little to remind the visitor of the building's antecedents, as it has been rebuilt several times, not only by the Portuguese but by their Dutch and British successors.

Bolgatty Palace *

Bolgatty Island, in the northern half of the bay, was chosen by the Dutch as their headquarters in Kochi. The residence of the Dutch East India Company (VOC) governor on the island was taken over by the British Resident after the Dutch were expelled. Built in 1744, the resi-

dent's 'palace' is now an eccentrically run hotel under the control of the Kerala Tourist Development Corporation. There are rumours, however, that it is to be taken over by a major Indian or international chain. There is no denying its character, and it is often used by Bombay-based film directors looking for a picturesque location. The Bolgatty Palace is also a good place to see **Kathakali**, the thrilling and theatrical traditional dance of Kerala and south India, in which elaborately costumed and gaudily painted dancers enact scenes from the great Hindu epics.

Above: *Kathakali dancers delight audiences with their elaborate costumes and vivid make-up.*

Periyar Wildlife Sanctuary *

A century ago, an artificial lake was formed by damming the **Periyar River**, in the midst of hill country some 190km (120 miles) east of Kochi. In the 1930s, the lake became the hub of a wildlife sanctuary which now covers some 780km² (300 sq miles). Wildlife is viewed by boat from the lake, and while **elephant** and **monkey** may be seen, the shyer animals – including the rare **tiger** for which the park is one of India's few havens – are often scared into hiding by the frequently noisy boatloads of visitors. The lake attracts a vast number of bird species. If you plan a visit, avoid weekends and Indian holidays, when the reserve is overcrowded and accommodation is usually full.

THE KERALA BACKWATERS

The boat journey through the enchanting Kerala backwaters is one of the main reasons for visiting the state. Fed by numerous streams and rivers flowing out of the eastern mountains, these backwaters are a vast expanse of lagoons and channels pent up behind the sand-bars of the coast. At points along the way the natural barrier between the freshwater channel and the open sea is so narrow that you can see the surf beyond it. Dotted with islands and fringed by palm plantations, the backwaters extend 80km (50 miles) or more from **Kollam** in the south to Alappuzha and **Kottayam** in the north, where they connect with the huge, brackish Vembanad Lake which opens into the sea at **Kochi**. Narrow channels and creeks meander from the main backwater lagoons into the countryside around, and tiny villages of fisher-folk and coir (coconut fibre) workers stand on the banks. The silver and green lakes and canals are busy with dozens of boats. They range from waddling, square-rigged rice barges to speedy, gondola-like snake-boats with high-powered outboard motors or tiny circular rafts made out of reeds, and the banks are lined with the skeletal gantries of Chinese-style fishing nets.

It is possible to make an extensive two- to three-day boat journey from Kochi to Kollam, but most people opt for the six- to eight-hour trip between Kollam and Alappuzha or the shorter two- to three-hour journey between Alappuzha and Kottayam. Several boats leave daily in each direction, operated by either the Kerala Tourist Development Corporation, local municipalities or some private operators. Tourist boats carry around 30 passengers even though the cabins and decks are rather small. They usually stop for lunch at one of the small villages en route and later tourists can have a swim in the lake.

PEOPLE OF THE BACKWATERS

The people of the Kerala backwaters live by fishing and by growing coconuts for coir, the rough fibre which is made into ropes and matting in Kochi and elsewhere. Fishing may be from boats or rafts or from the shore using the Chinese style nets which are also to be seen on the waterfront. Coconuts are husked and stacked neatly along the water's edge for collection by boat.

Kollam (Quilon)

Kollam is the southern jumping-off point for the backwaters, located about 120km (75 miles) south of Kochi. Close to the mouth of **Ashtamudi Lake**, which opens into the sea, Kollam itself is a place of no great interest, though there is an adequate beach at **Thangasseri**, 3km (2 miles) southeast of town.

Alappuzha (Alleppey)

Alappuzha, 45km (30 miles) south of Kochi, is a small but lively town criss-crossed by canals which link the northern channels of the backwaters with the southern end of **Vembanad Lake**. It is the northern terminus for the backwater trip. Boats also run through the canals to Vembanad Lake and Kottayam which is a picturesque shorter journey of roughly three hours. Real boat-travel fans can also continue to Kochi and Ernakulam via the lake.

Kottayam

Kottayam, the third gateway to the backwaters, is about 25km (15 miles) east of Alappuzha, and is linked with Vembanad Lake by its own system of waterways. Though of historic interest – St Thomas is said to have made converts here early in the Christian era – it offers no exciting sightseeing.

Above: *Heavy-laden rice barges make their slow way under sail through the backwater channels and lagoons.* **Opposite:** *Paddle-powered for a traditional race, snake-boats have outboard motors for everyday use.*

SPICES

Kerala produces most of the spices which combine to create Indian cuisine's piquant flavours. Most of India's **pepper**, 60% of its **cardamom** and almost all of its **ginger** – in fact, most of the world's ginger – is grown here. **Nutmeg** and **chillis** are also grown on the Kerala plantations.

Karnataka and Kerala at a Glance

BEST TIMES TO VISIT

Karnataka is perfect to visit from **November** to **February**, with daytime temperatures of 26°C to 30°C (79°F to 86°F) and low rainfall. **March** to **May** is uncomfortably hot and dusty. Rains begin in June–July and are at their heaviest in October.

GETTING THERE

Bangalore: there are two to three buses daily from Bijapur (8 hours), Bombay (24 hours plus), Ernakulam (10 hours); and 15 buses daily from Mysore (3 hours). Several trains run daily from Bombay, Bijapur, Hampi, Mysore and all points in central and southern India. One train runs daily from Vasco da Gama. Flights from Goa, Bombay and all major Indian cities.
Hampi: buses and trains are available from Goa, Vasco da Gama and Bangalore.
Bijapur: buses from Hampi (4 hours) and Bangalore (8 hours). Trains are also available from Hampi and Bangalore.
Frequent buses connect **Aihole**, **Pattadakal** and **Badami**. Badami is the best point for onward travel connections, with a daily bus (4 hours) and six trains (3½ hours) to Bijapur to the north and Hampi. The three sites can be explored by local bus, but for those with a little more money to spend the

best option is to take a taxi from Badami railway station. For travel to Mysore there are buses and trains from Bangalore and Kochi or Ernakulam (6 hours).
To get to **Trivandrum** take a bus from Kochi (6 hours). Flights from Bombay (2 hours 30 mins) and Bangalore (1 hour 30 mins) and international charter flights (12–13 hours) from London, Frankfurt and some other European airports. There are buses (8 hours) and trains from Bangalore to **Kochi**. Daily flights from Bangalore (1 hour), Trivandrum (30 mins) and several times daily to Bombay (2 hours 30 mins). Several trains and buses travel daily from Kochi (3–4 hours) and Trivandrum (1–2 hours) to **Kollam**. Buses and daily boats via the backwaters to Alappuzha. Frequent buses (2–3 hours) from Kollam and Kochi. To Alappuzha several trains daily (1–2 hours) from Ernakulam. Package tour passengers arriving at Trivandrum international airport are met by couriers and transfer coaches to get to **Kottayam**.
For independent travellers, there are buses approximately half-hourly from Trivandrum, taking less than 30 mins. Other options between Kottayam and Trivandrum include shared taxis and three-wheeled auto-rickshaws.

GETTING AROUND

Bangalore: taxis and auto-rickshaws within the city limits; taxis run to points outside the city limits. Car hire with driver available from major hotels.
Kochi/Ernakulam: Taxis and auto-rickshaws on land. Ferry network connects Ernakulam with Fort Kochi, Bolgatty and other islands. Motorboats can be hired from the pier on the mainland opposite the Bolgatty Palace.
Mysore: Taxis and auto-rickshaws. Car hire with driver available from main hotels and tour agencies.

WHERE TO STAY

Bangalore
LUXURY
Taj Residency Bangalore, 14 Mahatma Gandhi Road, tel: (080) 558 4444. Run by leading Indian chain.
The Oberoi Bangalore, 37–39 Mahatma Gandhi Road, tel: (080) 558 5858. Unquestionably the finest hotel in the city.

MID-RANGE
Ramanshree Comforts, 16 Rajaram Mohan Roy Road, tel: (080) 223 5250. New, comfortable mid-range hotel.
Bombay Anand Bhavan Hotel, 10 Grant Road, tel: (080) 221 4581. An affordable, friendly hotel.

Bijapur
BUDGET
Hotel Mayura Adil Shah,

Karnataka and Kerala at a Glance

Anand Mahal Road,
tel: 20934 (no codes, you
will have to go through the
operator). Comfortable,
cheap hotel run by the
**Karnataka State Tourism
Development Corporation**.
The annex has better rooms
and is quieter.

Mysore
LUXURY
**Ashok Radisson Lalitha
Palace Hotel**, Lalitha Palace
Road, tel: 27650 (no codes,
you will have to go through
the operator). Mysore's finest
luxury hotel is a landmark in
its own right, in a former
palace of the royal family.

BUDGET
Hotel Metropole, 5 Jhansi
Lakshmi Bai Road, tel: 20681
(no codes, you'll have to
go through the operator).
Splendid old-fashioned hotel
with fans and four-posters.
Excellent value for money.

Trivandrum
Most accommodation is
either in family homes, small
guesthouses or in new pack-
age-holiday hotels which are
usually fully booked by
European tour operators.

Kochi/Ernakulam
MID-RANGE
Taj Malabar Hotel,
Willingdon Island, tel:
340010 (no codes, you'll
have to go through the operator). Run by the Taj group,

Kochi's best hotel overlooks
the harbour and has a pool.

BUDGET
Bolgatty Palace Hotel,
Bolgatty Island, tel: 355003
(no codes, you'll have to go
through the operator). The
most atmospheric place to
stay in Kochi or Ernakulam.

Periyar Wildlife Sanctuary
MID-RANGE
The only available accommo-
dation is at the KTDC hotel,
formerly the Maharajah of
Travancore's Summer Palace.

WHERE TO EAT

Outside the larger cities listed
below, eating-places are
extremely basic and the most
reliable restaurants are those
in the hotels listed in the
Where to Stay section.

Bangalore
In Bangalore, there is a good
selection of restaurants
serving all kinds of Asian
and international cuisine.
Outside the main hotels –
most of which offer a choice
of European, Indian, and
Chinese or Japanese cuisine –
there is still plenty of choice.
Church Street, parallel to
Mahatma Gandhi Road,
offers a choice of places
to eat and drink, including
Coconut Grove, with open-
air tables, south Indian meals,
and draught beer. Across
the road, the **Nasa Pub** is a
Bangalore nightlife landmark.

Mysore
In Mysore the best value in
town is the barbecue on the
lawn at the **Hotel Metropole**, which also has an
excellent restaurant indoors.
The **Hotel Durbar** is good
value and its rooftop restaurant overlooks the city's park.

Trivandrum
Hotel restaurants are generally mediocre here, but the
small restaurant shacks which
line the beaches are excellent
value for money, especially
for seafood. Drinks are
expensive. These restaurants
close from June to September.

Kochi/Ernakulam
The classiest place to eat is
the waterfront terrace of the
Taj Malabar. The Bolgatty
Palace has a pleasant restau-
rant with a limited menu.

TOURS AND EXCURSIONS

In **Bangalore**, the **Karnataka
State Tourism Development
Corporation** tel: 212901 runs
tours every day to the main
sights. In **Mysore** the **KSTDC**
operates a range of city tours.
Periyar Wildlife Sanctuary:
Visit this as part of a tour organized by the KTDC which also
offers tours to Periyar itself.

USEFUL CONTACTS

Kerala Tourism, tel: 330031
(no codes available, please go
through the operator).
Karnataka Tourism Tours,
tel: 0175 2300.

8
Highlights of Maharashtra

Maharashtra, the state north of Goa, is one of the largest in India and offers huge contrasts. Its capital, **Bombay**, is for many the gateway to India. From the 17th century, it was the heartland of the Maratha empire, whose Hindu rulers successfully defied the power of the **Mughal** empire. The state is consequently dotted with the forts and castles of Maratha rulers. Among the important sightseeing attractions are Maharashtra's many cave temples, cut into the rock by earlier Buddhist, Jain and Hindu dwellers in the region. The most dramatic, at **Ajanta** and **Ellora**, rank among the world's most stunning ancient religious sites.

Maharashtra's Arabian Sea coast rises to the continental chain of the **Western Ghats** and the arid **Deccan** plateau. Travelling within the state is comparatively easy, with frequent air services between Bombay and places of interest, fast and comfortable express trains on key routes, and a good road network. During the British colonial era, hill stations of Maharashtra's mountain country were developed to provide the *sahibs* with relief from the summer heat of Bombay. Of these, **Pune** (Poona), **Mahabaleshwar** and **Matheran** are pleasantly temperate and have some old-fashioned charm.

Today, the state is an economic powerhouse, due to Bombay's thriving heavy and service industries and its huge import and export sector. As elsewhere in India, however, outside Maharashtra's bigger industrial cities rural life continues more or less untouched.

DON'T MISS

*** **Ellora:** complex of magnificently carved rock temples, more than a thousand years old.
*** **Ajanta:** more ancient cave temples, superbly decorated with frescoes and Buddha images.
** **Daulatabad:** grim hilltop fortress built more than six centuries ago. Awesome fortifications and spectacular location.

Opposite: *Carved Buddha images guard the entrance to the Ajanta cave temple complex in Maharashtra.*

AURANGABAD AND SURROUNDS

The main reason for visiting this city of 600,000, some 320km (200 miles) east of Bombay, is to see the wonderful cave temples at **Ajanta** and **Ellora** and the great Mughal stronghold at **Daulatabad**. Aurangabad also has some less distinguished cave temples of its own.

Aurangabad Caves *

About 4km (2½ miles) from the city centre and roughly 1km (⅔ miles) apart stand two groups of cave temples. They date from the later **Buddhist** era, and were built around the 7th century AD. The eastern caves, with their carved Buddha images, demigods and demons, are the most interesting.

Daulatabad **

The fortress of Daulatabad stands about 16km (10 miles) west of Aurangabad. The complex hilltop fortifications date from the 1320s, when the Sultan of Delhi, known as **Mohammed bin Tughlaq**, attempted to relocate his capital here, forcing the inhabitants of Delhi to move to the new site. The plan failed, and Daulatabad became a ghost fortress.

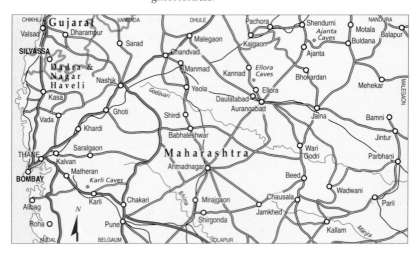

Left: *The vast Ellora cave complex is decorated with Buddhist, Hindu and Jain images carved into the cliff wall over a period of more than four centuries.*
Below: *Frescoes of the Buddha and his disciples illustrate the oldest Buddhist cave temples in India, at Ajanta.*

Ellora ★★★

The Ellora cave complex, about 30km (18 miles) north-west of Aurangabad, covers a 2km (1¼ miles) section of hillside and includes Buddhist, Hindu and Jain temples. The original complex comprises 34 caves, of which half are Hindu works, dating from the 9th century to the 13th century. A second cave complex, in the hills above Ellora, was found in 1990 and is being excavated. By far the most striking of them is the vast **Kailasha Temple**, the largest monolithic building in the world, elaborately carved with scenes from the **Mahabharata, Ramayana** and other Hindu epics. Other caves with finely preserved friezes include the Ramesvara, Dumar Lena and Dasa Avatara. Five **Jain rock temples** on the north side of the site are also worth looking at for their delicate sculptures.

Below: *Maharashtra women are traditionally among the most colourfully clad in India.*

Ajanta ★★★

The **Buddhist cave temples** at Ajanta, 100km (62 miles) northeast of Aurangabad, are among the oldest in India. They date from as early as the 2nd century BC when Buddhist monks settled here to begin the work of carving temples and sanctuaries from the walls of this rocky gorge. They were abandoned during the 7th century AD and rediscovered in 1819. The caves are decorated with **carvings** and gigantic **Buddha images**. The superb murals, painted in red, black, yellow and blue, depict scenes from the life of the Buddha and his disciples, and are even finer than the carvings.

PUNE (POONA) AND SURROUNDS

Now a busy modern city, Pune was a popular refuge from the Bombay heat during the British colonial era and still attracts people from Bombay, especially during the monsoon season. Pune also received worldwide recognition as it was the headquarters of the **Sri Baghwan Rajneesh** cult during the 1970s and '80s.

The 8th-century **Panchaleshwar Rock Temple** is similar to those at Ellora but is smaller and less impressive than its neighbours.

A splendidly eclectic private collection of artifacts and artworks, at the **Raja Kelkar Museum,** includes Hindu miniature paintings, arms and armour, musical instruments and furniture.

The wonderful 6ha (15 acre) **Gandhi National Memorial** garden surrounds the tomb of Kasturba Gandhi, the wife of India's great independence leader, who died here in 1944 while interned by the British. The Gandhis and other leaders of the 'Quit India' movement were interned in the former palace of the Aga Khan, which was given to the Indian government in 1969.

Maharashtra at a Glance

BEST TIMES TO VISIT

The more pleasant months in Maharashtra are from **December** through to **March**, when rainfall is minimal and maximum daytime temperatures are around 30°C (86°F). Avoid the hot, dry months of April and May, and the monsoon months of June to mid-October. Rainfall is heaviest in June and July, when there are daily downpours.

GETTING THERE

There are daily **flights** to **Aurangabad** from Bombay. The flights last for approximately one hour.
Buses are also available from Bombay (approximately 10 hours) as well as from Pune (roughly 5 hours). Frequent buses are available to **Daulatabad** from Aurangabad which will take about 30 minutes. Buses leave hourly from Aurangabad to the **Ajanta Caves** (3 hours).
There are half-hourly buses from Aurangabad to the **Ellora Caves** which is roughly a 30 minute trip. There are **flights** from Bangalore every day to **Pune**. The trip lasts for 2 hours. Several daily flights depart from Bombay every 45 mins. Several **trains** arrive daily from Bombay – the journey may last between 3 and 5 hours – and from Bangalore (24 hours).

GETTING AROUND

You can hire **taxis** and **auto-rickshaws** in both Aurangabad and Pune. **Cars** with driver can be hired by the day from larger hotels and from the Maharashtra State Tourism Development Corporation. In Pune, **bicycles** are available for rent at several smaller hotels.

WHERE TO STAY

Aurangabad
LUXURY
Ajanta Ambassador Hotel, Chikal Than, tel: 82211 (no codes available for hotels. Please ask the operator for help). Good value. Swimming pool facility.

Welcomegroup, Rama International, Rajendra Prasad Marg, tel: 82241. Top luxury hotel.

MID-RANGE
Aurangabad Ashok Hotel, Rajendra Prasad Marg, tel: 24520. Comfortable hotel, top of the mid-range sector.

Pune
MID-RANGE
Hotel Blue Diamond, Koregoan Park, tel: 28735. Comfortable hotel with luxuries including swimming pool and health club.

Hotel Saga Plaza, 1 Bund Garden Road, tel: 661880. Recently built mid-range hotel with pool.

Hotel Aurora Towers, 9 Moledina Road, tel: 641818. Pune's best hotel.

WHERE TO EAT

Aurangabad
Outside hotels, eating places are rather basic and mediocre. The Ajanta Ambassador's restaurants are highly recommended.

Pune
Moledina Road is lined with restaurants offering Indian cuisine, burgers and international menus.

For up-market dining, the **Aurora Towers Hotel** has a choice of international restaurants, Indian and Chinese cuisine.

TOURS AND EXCURSIONS

The **Maharashtra Tourist Development Corporation** (see Useful Contacts) operates excursions from Bombay to all the destinations and major sights. Destinations include the Ellora and Ajanta cave temples.

USEFUL CONTACTS

Indian Tourist Development Corporation, 123 Maharishi Karve Road, Bombay, tel: 291585.

Maharashtra Tourist Development Corporation, CDO Hutments, Madame Cama Road, Bombay, tel: (202) 6713.

Travel Tips

Tourist Information

The **Government of India Tourist Offices** handles all overseas information and promotion. Offices are at:
UK: 7 Cork Street, London W1X 2AB, tel: (0171) 734-6613.
USA: 30 Rockefeller Plaza, 15 North Mezzanine, New York NY 10112, tel: (212) 586-4901.
3550 Wilshire Boulevard, Suite 204, Los Angeles, CA 90010, tel: (213) 380-8855.
Canada: 60 Bloor Street West, Toronto, Ontario M4W 3B8, tel: (416) 962-6279.
Australia: Level 5, 65 Elizabeth Street, Sydney NSW 2000, tel: (02) 232-1600.
Within India: Information offices, tour itineraries and the Ashok hotel chain are operated at national level by the **Indian Tourism Development Corporation**, headquartered in New Delhi, and at state level by state tourism development corporations. ITDC HQ: 88 Janpath, New Delhi, tel: 332 0005.
Bombay and Maharashtra ITDC, 123 Maharishi Karve Road, Bombay, tel: 291585.

Maharashtra TDC, CDO Hutments, Madame Cama Road, Bombay tel: (202) 6713.
Goa ITDC, Communidade Building, Church Square, Panaji, tel: 3412.
Goa Directorate of Tourism, Tourist Home, Pato, Panaji, Goa, tel: 5620.
Karnataka ITDC, KFC Building, 48 Church Street, tel: 579517.
Karnataka State TDC, 10/4 Kasturba Road, tel: 212901.
Kerala ITDC, Willingdon Island, tel: 340352.
Kerala TDC, Tourist Reception Centre, Shanmugham Road, Ernakulam, tel: 353234.

Entry Requirements

All visitors require a visa. Tourist visas are normally valid for up to six months from date of issue. Visas must be issued by an Indian high commission or embassy before your departure. Visa issue can take up to two weeks and your passport must have two blank pages for the relevant stamps.
Indian Embassies, Consulates and High Commissions:
UK: India House, Aldwych, London WC2B 4NA, tel: (0171) 836-0990.
USA: 2107 Massachusetts Avenue, Washington DC 20008, tel: (202) 939-7000.
Australia: 3–5 Moonah Place, Yarralula, ACT 2600, tel: (06) 273-3999.
Canada: 10 Springfield Road, Ottawa, K1M 1C9, tel: (613) 744-3751.

Customs

You may import one litre of spirits or wine and 200 cigarettes. Hi-tech equipment such as video cameras or notebook computers should be registered on a tourist re-export form.

Health Requirements

Immunization against cholera, typhoid, polio, meningitis, hepatitis A and tetanus is strongly advisable. Take medical advice before travelling. Malaria is prevalent and a course of malaria prophylactics is essential. Take a good supply of mosquito repellent. Do not drink water unless it has been boiled and use water purifying tablets. Comprehensive health and accident insurance is essential.

Getting There

By Air: Main gateways for flights from the west are Bombay and New Delhi, with daily flights by Air India and other major airlines from most European capitals and from North America. Flight time from London is about 11 hours, and from New York, 19 hours. Air India and many other carriers also connect Bombay and New Delhi with major cities in Asia and Australasia.

There are frequent connecting flights to Goa by several domestic carriers, including Damania, East West Airlines, Indian Airlines, and Moduliluft, a partner of Lufthansa.

Direct charter flights to Goa and to Trivandrum operate from London and from several European airports during the tourist high season which is from September to April.

By Road: Long-distance buses connect Goa with Bombay, Bangalore, Mysore and other points in Karnataka and Maharashtra states. Long-haul bus travel is arduous.

By Rail: Express trains connect Goa's Vasco da Gama station with Bangalore and Mysore. From 1996 the Konkan coastal railway will provide through-train service to Bombay. Previously the rail journey from Bombay required a long detour inland via Miraj.

By Boat: A regular steamer service sails between Bombay and Goa. Sailing is suspended during the monsoon months.

What to Pack

Take the minimum amount of clothing for a Goan beach holiday. Shorts and T-shirts are all you will need at beach resorts. More modest clothing is required for sightseeing, visits to temples and churches, and any travel away from the beach.

Money Matters

Indian currency is the rupee, divided into 100 paisa and valued at approximately 40 rupees = £1 and 25 rupees = US$1.

Currency can be **exchanged** at banks in main cities and at your hotel. Retain currency conversion slips to reconvert rupees on your departure.

Traveller's cheques should be in sterling or in US dollars as it may be difficult to exchange other currencies. Credit cards are not widely accepted outside major hotels. When changing money, ask for some low-denomination notes and coins as rickshaw and taxi drivers often deny having change for larger notes.

Tipping is universal for all services, but there is no set percentage and a very small tip of a few rupees will usually suffice.

Accommodation

Goa and other tourist centres offer a wide range of accommodation, from extremely basic guesthouses catering to budget travellers to five-star luxury resorts and business hotels. Top range hotels in

India are surprisingly cheap by international standards.

While facilities match international levels, service standards may be more relaxed. Off the beaten track, accommodation can be extremely substandard, though also extremely cheap.

Eating Out

Only a tiny number of Indian people can afford to eat out or to eat anything but the simplest of meals.

Restaurants are therefore thin on the ground and concentrated in tourist areas and the business districts of Indian cities. In Goa, tiny, simple thatched restaurants line every beach, closing during the monsoon (when they are often partially demolished by high seas) to re-open with the beginning of the new tourist season. Don't expect a wide or sophisticated menu, though a choice of simpler international standards – such as burgers, steak and omelettes – is usually on offer. In Goa, seafood is really excellent.

Five-star **hotels** in major cities usually offer a choice of two or three restaurants –

usually a coffee-shop serving international meals, one or more restaurants serving traditional regional cuisine, as well as a Chinese or Japanese restaurant.

Small cafés, often called hotels, cater to Indian workers and travellers. The menu in these is usually very simple and meals are extremely cheap. A *thali*, a plated meal consisting of various kinds of *dal* (lentil) dishes, spicy vegetable dips, curds and yoghurt, is one of the best meals to order.

Beer and **wine** are luxury drinks in India, affordable only by the relatively wealthy, and most small cafés and restaurants which cater to ordinary Indians do not serve alcohol.

Transport

Air: The national carrier Indian Airlines operates a number of domestic routes in competition with several privately owned airlines including Modiluft, a partner of the German carrier Lufthansa; East West; Jet Airways; and Damania. Fares are very cheap by western standards, and considering the very long duration of land journeys air travel is often preferable. Internal air travel has become much safer in recent years, though Indian Airlines is still dogged by a poor safety reputation. Use the travel desk or travel agency in larger hotels to handle the booking for you. **Trains:** India's rail network is one of the world's largest. The **class** system is complicated, comprising air condi-

tioned (A/C) and non A/C 1st class, A/C sleeper and chair car, 2nd class sleeper, reserved-seat 2nd class, and unreserved 2nd class. Fares are very cheap. Unreserved 2nd class is always incredibly crowded and should be avoided wherever possible. Rail travel can be **booked** via a hotel, tour agency or at Indian Railways computerized booking offices, found in the departure hall of even the small main stations.

The Indrail Pass, sold by Indian Railways, allows travel on any train for periods of 24 hours, and 7, 15, 30, 60 or 90 days. It is sold by sales agents worldwide.

Bombay has two long-distance railway stations. Central Railways trains go from **Victoria Terminus** (renamed Chatrapati Shivaji Maharaj Terminus) close to the Fort area of town, which handles trains to Karnataka, Maharashtra and onward connections to Goa, as well as services to Madhya Pradesh, Uttar Pradesh, Haryana, and Rajasthan. **Central Station,**

north of the city centre, handles Western Railway services to Agra and New Delhi, Rajasthan and Gujarat.

Vasco da Gama is the main station for Goa, with rail connections only to Karnataka. A new railway line, the Konkan, is scheduled to open in late 1996, connecting Goa with the Maharashtra coast to the north and the Karnataka coast to the south. Aurangabad, Pune, Bijapur, Bangalore, Mysore, Kochi, Kollam and Trivandrum all have mainline rail services.
Buses: Long distance buses link Goa with all the surrounding states. Fares are very low, but so are standards of comfort. Bus travel should be a last resort.
Taxis: Ordinary taxis are black with a yellow roof. Theoretically they are metered, but the appearance of a foreigner frequently causes mysterious meter malfunctions. Insist on the meter, agree a fare before boarding, or find another driver.
Auto-rickshaws: Hybrids of motor-scooter and chariot,

CONVERSION CHART		
FROM	TO	MULTIPLY BY
Millimetres	Inches	0.0394
Metres	Yards	1.0936
Metres	Feet	3.281
Kilometres	Miles	0.6214
Kilometres square	Square miles	0.386
Hectares	Acres	2.471
Litres	Pints	1.760
Kilograms	Pounds	2.205
Tonnes	Tons	0.984
To convert Celsius to Fahrenheit: x 9 ÷ 5 + 32		

with a bench-seat for two mounted behind the driver and partially enclosed by a canopy. Like taxis, they are supposed to be metered but fares are almost always a matter of haggling. In many places, 'auto' drivers speak very little English.

Car hire: Self-drive car hire is not recommended because of the many peculiar hazards of Indian motoring. Cars with drivers can be hired by the day from top hotels, travel agencies, TDC offices and car rental outlets.

Motorcycles: Motorcycles can be hired in several Goan beach resorts. Maintenance and safety standards are shaky and helmets are not usually provided. Do not rent unless you are familiar with motorbikes and have a sound mechanical knowledge.

Business Hours

Banks open from 10:00–14:00 Monday–Friday and 10:00–12:00 Saturday. Post offices open from 10:00–17:00 weekdays and 10:00–12:00 Saturdays. Many **shops** in Goa close from around midday until late afternoon. Because of its many different faiths, India has a huge calendar of regional and national religious festivals, during which most shops and offices are closed.

Time Difference

GMT + 5 hrs 30 mins.

Communications

Indian **postal** services are slow but reliable. Most holiday hotels sell stamps. International direct-dial **phone** and **fax** facilities can be found in most holiday hotels. You may have to wait for some time for even local calls to be connected. The code situation in India is extremely complicated. Only major cities have direct dial, elsewhere all calls must go through the operator. Even if direct dial is available, many numbers aren't available by direct dial and only through the operator. Metered phones and faxes are available in STD/ISD booths in tour

agencies, shops and other businesses throughout India.

A government-run 24-hour STD/ISD phone and fax centre operates in Bombay: Videsh Sanchar Bhavan, Mahatma Gandhi Road, Bombay 400 001, tel: (022) 204 2728. Be warned, though, that thousands of telephone numbers go out of date every year and so some of the numbers given in this guide will have been changed at the time of going to press. The number for Directory Enquiries is 191 and the international code for India is 00 91.

Electricity

230–240 volts AC, two-pin sockets.

Weights and Measures

India uses the **metric** system of weights and measures.

Health Precautions

It is essential that you take comprehensive health precautions and medical advice before travelling to India and many inoculations must be administered several weeks before departure.

Comprehensive medical **insurance**, which should include emergency repatriation, is a must. Do not drink **tap water** anywhere in India unless you have boiled or sterilized it yourself. Carry water sterilizing tablets, available from chemists in the UK and elsewhere, and a water bottle if you are heading off the beaten track where bottled drinks may not be available.

Food is not safe anywhere in India, even in luxury hotels. In general, you just have to trust your own judgement as to whether a restaurant looks acceptably clean. Many travellers choose to avoid meat completely in India, and cooked vegetarian food may pose fewer health risks .

Malaria is present in southern India. Your doctor will prescribe the appropriate prophylactics, but the best way to avoid malaria is to avoid being bitten by mosquitoes. A repellent containing a high percentage of *deet*, diethyl toluamide, can be applied to skin, hair or clothing and is effective. Mosquito nets can be bought in specialist travel shops abroad or on arrival in India.

Sunburn and heat exhaustion are significant risks. Minimize

GOOD READING

• Scott, Paul (1975) *The Raj Quartet*. Penguin, London.
• Rushdie, Salman (1992) *The Satanic Verses*. The Consortium, Inc. London and New York.
• Naipaul, V. S (1991) *India: A Million Mutinies Now*. Minerva, London.
• Allen, Charles (1975) *Plain Tales from the Raj*. ed. Charles Allen Futura, London.
• Moorhouse, Geoffrey (1986) *India Britannica*. Paladin London.
• Spear, Percival (1975) *A History of India*. Pelican, London.

time spent in the sun and cover up. Take plenty of non-alcoholic fluids to avoid dehydration. Beware of infection in small cuts and scrapes: wash carefully and apply an antiseptic ointment or cream.

Health Services

Most five-star hotels have a doctor on call. In emergencies, private clinics offer a faster response than general hospitals. Your insurance must include an emergency repatriation option.

Personal Safety

Incidents of violent crime are very rare but **theft** is not uncommon. Do not leave passports, cash, travellers cheques, travel documents or other valuables in your room. Carry them with you or put them in the hotel safe.

Possessions left unattended on the beach are especially vulnerable. Keep a close watch on your possessions when travelling by train. Reporting theft to the police is a time-consuming bureaucratic process.

Use of soft **drugs**, especially marijuana is widespread among young budget travellers to Goa. The authorities believe drug use can be stamped out by imposing severe penalties, including 10-year jail sentences, for possession of even small amounts.

You may be approached by drug dealers. Be cautious and aware that many of

them double as police informers or may even be plainclothes policemen.

Emergencies
Ambulance: Bombay, tel: 102; Goa, tel: 5926/2211.
Police: tel: 100.

Etiquette

Indians value modesty. Beachwear is acceptable at beach resorts, far less acceptable elsewhere, and wholly unacceptable in churches, mosques, temples and national monuments.

Remove shoes on entering places of worship. If travelling on business, jacket and tie for men and formal business attire for women are the norm; even on holiday, you will find dealing with Indian officialdom (in post offices, police stations, railway booking offices and other situations) easier if you are less informally dressed.

Topless sunbathing and nudity are tolerated on some Goan beaches, but arouse intense curiosity among Indian visitors.

Language

India is a land of many different languages. There are 15 major languages as well as hundreds of dialects. Although Hindi is the official national language, it is not really that widely spoken in southern India.

Throughout India, English is spoken everywhere: in shops, offices and hotels and by almost all educated Indians.

INDEX

INDEX

PLACENAMES IN INDIA

Some of the names of places in India have recently, or over recent years, been changed back to their original Indian names. The following list gives the previous and current names of the main places affected in this book. The names adopted in the book are marked below with an asterisk.

PREVIOUS NAME	CURRENT NAME
Bombay*	Mumbai
Calicut*	Kozhikode
Cochin	Kochi*
Panjim	Panaji*
Poona	Pune*
Quilon	Kollam*
Trivandrum*	Thiruvanathapuram
Victoria Terminus* (Bombay)	Chatrapati Shivaji Maharaj Terminus